Frigatebirds, Sea Lions, and Darwin

Frigatebirds, Sea Lions, and Darwin

Musings on Evolution, Creation, and Ecology

David B. Schreiner

WIPF & STOCK · Eugene, Oregon

FRIGATEBIRDS, SEA LIONS, AND DARWIN
Musings on Evolution, Creation, and Ecology

Copyright © 2025 David B. Schreiner. All rights reserved. Except for brief quotations in critical publications or reviews, no part of this book may be reproduced in any manner without prior written permission from the publisher. Write: Permissions, Wipf and Stock Publishers, 199 W. 8th Ave., Suite 3, Eugene, OR 97401.

Wipf & Stock
An Imprint of Wipf and Stock Publishers
199 W. 8th Ave., Suite 3
Eugene, OR 97401

www.wipfandstock.com

PAPERBACK ISBN: 979-8-3852-0317-8
HARDCOVER ISBN: 979-8-3852-0318-5
EBOOK ISBN: 979-8-3852-0319-2

VERSION NUMBER 03/28/25

To my traveling companions, Ginny, Maddie, Bailey, and Lily.
I am forever grateful for our adventures.

To Sandra Richter and Lawson Stone.
You pushed me to think about creation more deeply.

To Ben Brammell.
I hope our conversations have helped you
as much as they've helped me.

Contents

List of Illustrations | ix
Preface | xiii

1. The Difficulty of Travel and Humanity | 1
2. The Islands Born of Fire | 18
3. Social Media, Genesis, and Intentions | 30
4. Genesis 1–11: What's Going on Here? | 46
5. Seal Lions Bites and Frigatebirds | 64
6. A Sleeping Lion and a Changing World | 81
7. Water Ferries, Economics, and the Problem with Tourists | 94
8. Wrapping Up These Musings | 105

Bibliography | 117

List of Illustrations

Figure 1: Map of the Galápagos Islands <https://creativecommons.org/licenses/by-sa/3.0>, via Wikimedia Commons | xvi

Figure 2: HMS Beagle Diagram; HTO, public domain, via Wikimedia Commons | 7

Figure 3: HMS Beagle at Tierra del Fuego; "HMS Beagle at Tierra del Fuego" by Conrad Martens (1801–21 August 1878), public domain, via Wikimedia Commons | 8

Figure 4: *The Creation of Adam*; Michelangelo, public domain, via Wikimedia Commons | 12

Figure 5: Nazca Plate; edits by Ingo Wölbern, public domain, via Wikimedia Commons | 19

Figure 6: Ocean Currents; US army, public domain, via Wikimedia Commons | 20

Figure 7: *Wall of Tears*; photo by David B. Schreiner | 24

Figure 8: Lonesome George; https://www.flickr.com/photos/mikeweston/, CC BY 2.0 <https://creativecommons.org/licenses/by/2.0>, via Wikimedia Commons | 26

List of Illustrations

Figures 9–10: Screenshots of Ken Ham's Twitter Posting, June 12, 2023. | 33–34

Figure 11: Tablet from the Baal Cycle; Louvre Museum, CC BY-SA 2.0 FR <https://creativecommons.org/licenses/by-sa/2.0/fr/deed.en>, via Wikimedia Commons | 42

Figure 12: Tablet 11 from Gilgamesh Epic, Also Known as Flood Tablet; photograph by Mike Peel (www.mikepeel.net)., CC BY-SA 4.0 <https://creativecommons.org/licenses/by-sa/4.0>, via Wikimedia Commons | 57

Figure 13: Sea Lions on a Beach on San Cristóbal; photo by David B. Schreiner | 65

Figure 14: Sea Lions on Playa Mann; photo by David B. Schreiner | 66

Figure 15: Galápagos Sea Lions Lying on Playa Mann; photo by David B. Schreiner | 69

Figure 16: A Galápagos Sea Lion Relaxing in the Sun: photo by David B. Schreiner | 72

Figure 17: Frigatebird Flying; photo by David B. Schreiner | 75

Figure 18: Frigatebird Overlooking Cerro Brujo; photo by David B. Schreiner | 77

Figure 19: Kicker Rock; photo by David B. Schreiner | 82

Figure 20: A Pacific Green Sea Turtle; photo by David B. Schreiner | 83

Figure 21: A Marine Iguana on Cerro Brujo; photo by David B. Schreiner | 85

Figure 22: Two Marine Iguanas; photo by David B. Schreiner | 87

Figure 23: Blue Footed Boobies, Galápagos Penguins, Galápagos Sea Lions in the Bay of Villamil; photo by David B. Schreiner | 89

List of Illustrations

Figure 24: Galápagos Penguins; MasterfulNerd, CC BY-SA 4.0 <https://creativecommons.org/licenses/by-sa/4.0>, via Wikimedia Commons | 92

Figure 25: Water Taxis on Isabela; photo by David B. Schreiner | 97

Figure 26: A Marine Iguana Lying on Lava Rocks with Some Sally Lightfoot Crabs; photo by David B. Schreiner | 100

Figure 27: A Galápagos Tortoise Crossing the Road Outside of El Chato Ranch on Santa Cruz; photo by David B. Schreiner | 109

Preface

I HAVE WRITTEN THIS with a fair amount of trepidation. It's different from the type of stuff I normally write. I am most comfortable with detailed and technical research into primary sources of biblical studies or analyses of ancient cultures. Here I have exchanged those comforts for a series of critical reflections that, while dealing with things of biblical interpretation, also forced me to consider things of biology, evolution, and ecology. Moreover, the impetus of this work is not some interpretive question or historical problem, such has been the case in my past work. Rather, it was born out of family vacations, perpetual discussions with family members, and a desire to discuss shifting positions on very complex topics.

I'm also anxious about this work because I am just another voice in a very crowded room. I will touch upon this in the opening chapters, but the reality is that it's very trendy, or has been in recent memory, for Christians to write on issues of creation, evolution, and ecology. There are several reasons for this, and I certainly don't want to get into that discussion here. However, I do think that there is more to be said about the difficulty that Christians have with these conversations, particularly since they involve non-Christian scientists. Based on the discussions that I have had over the years, I really do think that many scientists think that Christian conversations about evolution, creation, and ecology are handicapped by certain assumptions that we embrace. Of course I am speaking in generalities here, and of course there are notable exceptions, but there's a point when Christians who want to have these large-scale conversations about evolution, ecology, and biology need to accept that we are often the recipients of veiled and exaggerated eye-rolling. I tried to engage this reality at various points.

The transparency of this work is another reason why this project makes me nervous. At various places you will read about the development of my positions. You will hear about how I grew up, where I grew up, and how I have deviated from my intellectual and theological heritage. And perhaps most significantly, you will sense how I am moving, with increasing clarity, to the middle of the political spectrum on the issues that I discuss in the pages that follow. Ultimately, though, I am OK with this, and above all I hope it will model for my daughters what honest critical reflection does for a person.

Speaking of family, a huge thanks must go to my brother-in-law. We have had countless conversations on these things. From my perspective, each one—without exception—has been well worth the time and energy invested in it, particularly since we both teach at Christian institutions of higher education. You will read about these in the pages that follow, but I am grateful for how they have encouraged me to be more precise, look for nuance, and be honest. He is a very smart guy that also has a very interesting intellectual journey on these topics. I wish he would share it more. But alas, that's a story for him to tell.

I am also grateful for my traveling companions: Ginny, Maddie, Bailey, and Lily. You will read about our adventures in the pages that follow. But you will also read about the lessons I have learned in the wake of those adventures. Traveling adventures are emotionally powerful because they create a bond in the family. However, they are even more powerful when those emotions and memories are tied to lessons learned. So, I must say thank you to all of them for the experiences, memories, bonds, and lessons.

Preface

I hope and pray this book helps someone. It helped me. The conversations here are neither simple nor fleeting. My positions will almost certainly continue to change, but I pray that I can continue to be honest in what needs to be assessed and admitted.

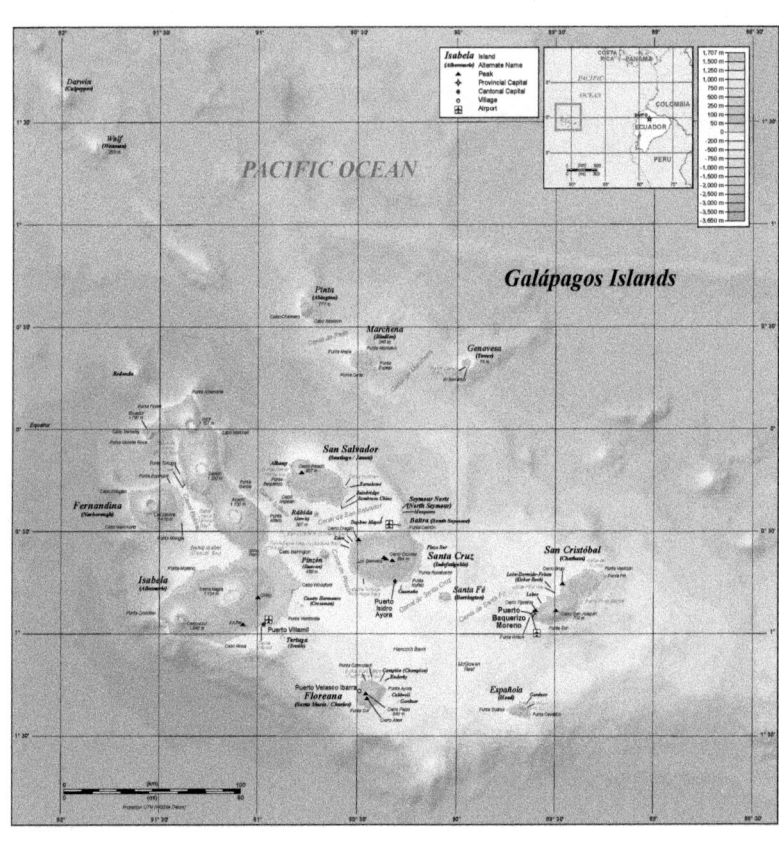

1

The Difficulty of Travel and Humanity

IN THE UNITED STATES of America, travel is relatively easy. Between the copious number of rental car agencies, airline options, the sprawling interstate system, and (in certain regions) public transportation, people can make decisions on a whim to travel hundreds or even thousands of miles to visit something on their bucket list. However, the difficulty of traveling increases when certain variables come into the equation. For example, are you traveling domestically or internationally? In the case of the former, save for the impending requirement of the "Real ID," the amount of documentation necessary is really not that big of a deal. If you've got money and a valid form of identification, and as long as you're not on a "no-fly" list (for whatever reason), you can fly. To rent a car, you just need a valid driver's license and a method of payment. If you're traveling by air, the amount of connecting flights for domestic travel is usually manageable. Yet, if you are traveling internationally, you do have to account for passports, multiple connections (usually), immigration forms, and more. During the COVID-19 pandemic, we all remember the added variable of each country's immunization and testing requirements. These issues notwithstanding, traveling with kids is, at least in my opinion, the single most anxiety-producing variable, particularly when travel involves navigating airports. Whether domestic or international, if you are traveling with kids, your blood pressure will spike—and stay spiked. Your nerves will be frayed. Your exhaustion level will explode, which also means that you will likely get into an arguments with your family.

I remember traveling with my kids several years ago to Mississippi. Because I was living in central Kentucky and worked for Wesley Biblical Seminary, an independent seminary in the Wesleyan holiness tradition rooted in the Jackson, Mississippi, metro area, I had to make the nine- or ten-hour trek by car a handful of times per year to convince my employers that I was still alive and producing for the institution. In this case, my family came with me. Overall, it was a decent trip. But I do remember that at one point, when the trip time had eclipsed ten hours, there was a potty emergency.

"Daddy! I've got to go potty!"

"Can it wait?"

"*No!* I'm gonna pee my pants! Real bad! I've got to go *real bad!*"

So, I did what any good dad would do. I pulled the car off the shoulder of Interstate 55 South and exposed my middle child's bottom, holding her up so she wouldn't pee all over herself. There were some horns that honked as they drove by, but the task was accomplished. We could proceed and finish the final forty miles or so and get to Jackson.

Unfortunately, this was not the end of things. No more than ten miles later:

"Daddy. I've got to go potty."

"No, you just went."

With an increasing amount of anxiety, "Daddy, I've got to go. I can't wait."

If you have kids, then you probably know what happened next. I tried my best to ignore what was happening. There was no way I was stopping. We had just stopped, and my child could hold it. Besides, we were almost to our destination. Unfortunately, the cries from the back just kept getting more intense and more frequent. And then came the look from Ginny (my wife). She didn't say anything, but the look said, "Just pull over and let her go again." So, I pulled to the right of I-55 one more time to revisit the course of action that was no more than fifteen minutes old.

During the Christmas season of 2022, Ginny and I were enjoying a nice evening bagel at Panera. We were sitting in front of their fireplace talking about her travel goals for 2023. There, she said that she really wanted to go to Galápagos Islands to meet her brother on vacation. Now, we had traveled to England, Scotland, and other places. So, there was part of me that was not surprised by this. But this was the Galápagos Islands. Not only were they the property of Ecuador, a developing country in South America, but there were also six hundred miles off the coast of Ecuador. Consequently, it goes without saying that this was a next-level request. Moreover, it became clear that the best course of action to realize this goal was to bring the kids. The length of the trip effectively precluded pawning our kids off to a relative, and I wasn't going to sit back and watch Ginny with my oldest daughter (almost twelve at the time) navigate foreign countries and airports. It's not that Ginny couldn't do it; she had been to Africa before. But I couldn't handle it. It would have wrecked my nerves. Nevertheless, this conversation represented a significant intensification of the Schreiner-family vacation philosophy. But in the end, the decision was made. The Schreiners would be headed to a new continent to engage a foreign culture for the payoff of sea lions, snorkeling, and other tropical activities.

Now some of you reading this may be seasoned travelers. You may be thinking, "Oh, that's not that bad." However, by the number of times I had to answer questions of who exactly was going and who was watching the kids, I am guessing that a majority of people would empathize with the anxiety that was building week by week, day by day, as the trip approached. "Spanish? How much can I remember from Señior Collins' Spanish classes at Continental Local High School? When I was in Mexico, I had translators with me . . . all the time. I don't think Maddie's Duolingo lessons will help her function as our interpreter . . ."

But my anxiety was associated with things other than just the language barrier that awaited us. In order to keep our airfare low, we booked a flight with several connections. So I thought, "What if we miss our connection? How will the kids respond to that . . . to all that waiting?" According to the original flight, we were going to have to spend a nine-hour layover in the Quito airport, sleeping on benches as we waited for the Consejo de Gobierno del Regimen Especial de Galápagos to open.

You see, to get to the Galápagos Islands, it's logistically complicated. You have to funnel through either Quito or Guayaquil for a layer of entry fees and biosecurity screening. What's biosecurity screening? It's a process whereby you and your luggage—both checked and carry-on—are scanned to prevent invasive species and compounds from entering the Galápagos ecosystem. A security team scans and X-rays your luggage and then seals it to ensure that no unwanted synthetic or organic material enters. This means that a long layover is usually inevitable. But nine hours? Sleeping on benches? With three girls all ages twelve or younger?

Another source of anxiety came in the form of juvenile annoyances. I find it annoyingly interesting how kids can sniff out in-flight entertainment. For example, our middle daughter (the only who just *had* to go potty along the highway in Mississippi) observed a rather small QR code on the back of our airbus seats and immediately began interrogating me about what it was. These were the directions on how to access the in-flight entertainment, but I was not going to volunteer that information. Ginny and I still believe that constant access to technology contributes to spastic behavior and short attention spans. However, we all have our breaking points. So, when Bailey wouldn't stop answering my vague and curt answers with more penetrating questions, I relented and let her hijack my Samsung Galaxy S20 Note to watch *Encanto* and other movies of that ilk. The only condition was that she had to share with her sisters.

Don't worry. Ginny and I aren't uncouth Neanderthals.

Food is another variable that makes traveling with kids potentially maddening. Our three healthy and growing daughters are always hungry. So, whether we are walking through a terminal or sitting on the plane mid-flight, their eyes quickly focus on anything that looks good. In case of Lily, our six-year-old, she'll usually say something like, "I wish I could have that, but it's too expensive." You see, Ginny and I have trained them well. Airport food is like ballpark food. It's overpriced and really not that good. You just don't buy it. Instead, you bring your own. Nevertheless, kids are bottomless pits. They will eventually eat everything that you brought, and at that point, the volleys of statements declaring their hunger will commence.

On May 28, 2023, the Schreiners started the first leg of what became our first journey to Ecuador by flying to Ft. Meyers, Florida. The plan was to fly in, rent a car, and slowly make our way to Miami International Airport, where we would be leaving the country. The path would take us from Miami on May 30th to Bogota to Quito and finally to San Cristóbal by way of Guayaquil. However, as soon as we arrived at the Miami airport, we hit our first snag.

A few days prior, LATAM Airlines sent me an email informing me that critical information was needed for our flight. I knew, essentially, what this was. They needed the typical passenger information along with passport numbers and a few other things. Yet when I clicked on the link to enter that information, I kept receiving an error message. Consequently, all that information would be needed at the check-in counter. However, when I approached the counter, I was immediately shooed back to a kiosk. This seemed fine, but when I encountered a similar error message to the one I had been receiving through the app on my phone, my blood pressure started to rise. Thankfully, there was a nice lady there to assist. But, alas, she was ultimately no help. She couldn't navigate past the error messages. Therefore, she ushered us back to the check-in counter.

After I explained to them why I returned, the pleasant lady behind the counter smiled and understood the situation. But then she turned to me and asked a simple question:

"Where are you going?"

"Bogota. Then to Quito and San Cristóbal."

There was typing. Then she looked at me.

"You're not on that flight to Bogota."

"What?"

"You're not on the flight."

I had been here before. A few years prior, Delta Airlines struck me from my flight out of Mexico City. It was Easter weekend, and there were no flights back to the United States until the next day. In that case, however, it was just me. Here and now, I was with my family who had been chomping at the bit for weeks to get to the islands.

I just stared at her in disbelief. So, she returned to searching. And after what seemed like hours, she looked up and said, "You're not on the flight to Bogota, but you're on a flight to Quito."

"Wait. So we are going straight to Quito? There's no Bogota? Why wasn't I told this? I have no email telling me this."

This should have been welcomed with open arms. I mean, to have one less connection, that's good, right? However, this unplanned adjustment meant that the nine-hour layover in Quito became fifteen. Waiting around the Quito airport for fifteen hours was going be a problem.

I am pleased to report that our LATAM flight to Quito went off without a problem. The biggest problem was the expectations surrounding in-flight meals and snacks. Apparently, our children expected hamburgers, fries, and chicken nuggets. So, when the ham and cheese wraps were distributed, Ginny and I chuckled at their dejection. Also, it must be acknowledged that the fifteen-hour layover in Quito was excellent. We broke down and booked a night at the Wyndham at the Quito airport. Moreover, the multiple hurdles involved with biosecurity, taxes, check-ins, and the forty-minute stop in Guayaquil on the way to San Cristóbal offered no problems. When we arrived at the San Cristóbal airport, we were corralled into the hot terminal to pay even more taxes for use of the National Park and watched our luggage get sniffed by dogs trained to identify contraband. Once all of this was done, we were free to meet Uncle Ben and see the sights of the island.

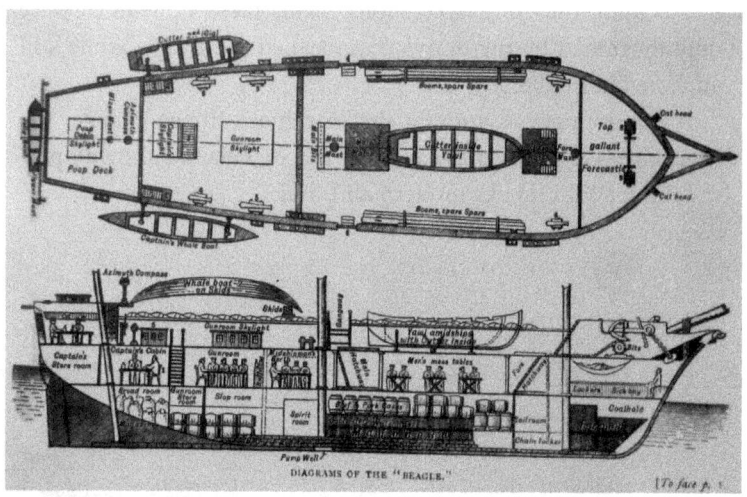

Diagram of the HMS Beagle, the Ship that Took
Darwin to the Galápagos Islands.

I can only imagine what it was like for Charles Darwin as he traveled on the HMS Beagle toward the Galápagos Islands and beyond. At twenty-two, poised not to become the father of modern biology but rather a mundane clergyman, Darwin enthusiastically accepted the appointment as a naturalist on the Beagle's second exploratory campaign. It was a modest ship that was described by Darwin on multiple occasions as "crowded." In a letter to Susan Darwin, he declared that "the want of room is very bad."[1] About a month later, Darwin moaned to J. S. Henslow, "[My] corner of the cabin is woefully small."[2] Such cramped quarters apparently also exacerbated negative personality traits. For example, in the same letter to J. S. Henslow, Darwin refers to his "friend the Doctor" as an "ass."[3] Robert FitzRoy, the captain of the Beagle, was apparently known for his "incandescent temper" and was apparently prone

1. Darwin, "Letter No. 126."
2. Darwin, "Letter No. 144."
3. Darwin, "Letter No. 144."

to storming out of conversations.⁴ And these difficulties were only magnified by the delays that plagued the Beagle while still anchored in England.

Interestingly, it appears that the more things change, the more they stay the same. Crowded spaces, delays, annoying personalities all sound like modern air travel.

"HMS Beagle at Teirra del Fuego" by Conrad Martens.

But the hurdles went beyond logistics and accommodations. Darwin testifies to a cholera quarantine that prevented him from disembarking the Beagle to see Teneriffe, the largest of the Canary Islands.⁵ Also, Darwin was perpetually seasick on his five-year voyage.⁶ In virtually all of his early correspondences, he bemoaned

---

4. Johnson, *Darwin*, 26
5. Darwin, *Voyage*, 11.
6. Analyses of Darwin's ill health, both during his voyage and throughout his life, are well known. See, for example, Botto-Mahan and Medel, "Was Chagas Disease," 1–7; Campbell and Matthews, "Darwin's Illness Revealed," 248–51; Colp Jr., *Darwin's Illness*; Orrego and Quintana, "Darwin's Illness," 23–29; Sheehan et al., "More on Darwin's Illness," 205–9; Young, "Darwin's Illness," 77–86.

The Difficulty of Travel and Humanity

the seasickness that plagued him. Indeed, by the early months of 1832, Darwin celebrated that he felt as if he had turned a corner, but later letters recount the return of his bouts with seasickness.[7] Most significantly, it appears that as he traveled around the south and west tips of South America, he became significantly sick at least twice. In October of 1833, a fever forced him to abandon his travels on land,[8] and in July of 1834, he was bedridden for a month.[9] There were also inevitable storms, mechanical problems, and natural disasters such as earthquakes and volcanic eruptions. Nevertheless, there are interludes in his correspondences that emphatically proclaim that all the hardship paled in comparison to the beauty of the natural world.

So, what's the point of all of this? Why am I interlacing stories about my family's travels with conversations about Darwin and his travels? This work targets the convergence of science, passages in the Bible, and Christian theology. But this not only gets technical and boring very quickly, but it's also a well-trodden trail. In fact, within recent memory, there has been a boom in Christians weighing in on these topics in a variety of ways, whether it be on issues of creation care in general or, more generally, on the relationship between Christian theology and science (I will interact with some of these below). This is the result of a rather complicated trend that considers political sentiments and theology with a deepening understanding of humanity's origins and environmental impact. Yet the distinctiveness of this work is twofold. First, the experiences of my family between May and June of 2023 and then again between May and June of 2024 are the mechanisms that will spur diffuse thoughts about Christian theology, environmentalism, and science. I am sharing our experiences to possibly produce similar reflections in the minds of my readers. If anything, this work may

---

7. Darwin, "Letter No. 159." See also Darwin, "Letter No. 158."
8. Darwin, "Letter No. 259."
9. Darwin, "Letter No. 251."

be a welcome change of pace to conversations that quickly become technical and even idiosyncratic.

Secondly, this work aims to be cathartic. I grew up in a conservative, fundamentalist home as the son of a conservative United Methodist pastor. We took the Bible seriously. We read the Bible "literally." Therefore, the default position on issues of creation and ecology was that God miraculously created the world in a week, and humanity enjoyed a privileged place in that creation. As for issues of ecology, it was just not a point of emphasis. Rather, the overwhelming concern when reading the Bible revolved around issues of personal salvation. Essentially, humanity was the apex of God's creative actions and therefore wanted to see us back in communion with him. By implication it seemed that humanity's relationship with the environment was only an issue if it contributed to conversations about the salvation of humanity. And if it did come up in the midst of any political discourse, it was quickly dismissed as "stuff that Democrats and tree huggers care about."

Now, make no mistake, I am grateful for the way I was raised. The emphasis upon Scripture, its authority, is something that I continue to hold and even pass on to my kids. Moreover, I have come to echo the emphasis that the salvation of humanity is at the heart of the Christian faith. If you are beginning to think that I'm ashamed of my conservative upbringing or that I was compelled to "deconstruct" the faith of my parents and childhood, please stop. I only mean to say that I have come to realize that the points of emphasis that functioned as the pillars of the Schreiner household did not tell the whole story. What was missed was a realization that a robust understanding of the opening chapters of Genesis *requires* that we come to grips with humanity's place in the created order, particularly because everything is so flawed and broken. To put it theological terms, soteriology demands an ecological awareness. Moreover, I have come to realize that the conversations about creation, the message of Gen 1–3, and humanity's place within the created order are really complicated and continue to be ripe with contention. So, it's my hope that the catharsis found in this book may resonate with some of you.

This latter objective was crystallized as I reflected upon a telling conversation I had with my brother-in-law as we stood at the Playa de la Estacion near the Darwin Research Center on Santa Cruz. It was a conversation about modern ecological theory and the creation care often advocated by Christians. Ben, who is a biology professor, proceeded to tell me that many scientists engage ecology with a perspective that seeks to restrict human activity as much as possible. He explained it via a series of premises:

- Premise 1: Humans have been present on earth for only about 0.14 percent of the history of life on earth (life on earth for 3.7 billion and humans for perhaps 5 million).

- Premise 2: Humans have done far more to destroy the world's ecosystems than any species that came before.

- Premise 3: The central goal of ecology based on contemporary conservation efforts is to ameliorate, as much as possible, the destructive impact of humans and preserve natural areas from future impacts ("natural," in this context, is defined as areas not impacted by humans).

- Premise 4: So, the role of humans is to restore as much of the natural world as possible to the state in *which it evolved in the absence of human influence.*

This final phrase, ". . . in which it evolved in the absence of human influence," is most interesting to me. According to Ben, impactful conservation values the state of things prior to humanity's existence. Essentially, it seeks ecological restoration.[10] If this is

---

10. According to McConnell and Abel, ecological restoration is the antidote to an anthropological self-centeredness that has culminated in scarcity of resources:

> It is an understatement to say that [the days where humans have a negligible impact upon the environment] are long gone. According to environmental philosopher and provocateur Garrett Hardin, the post-hunter-gatherer human approach became *exploit, ruin, move-on*, which was based on the mistaken assumption that the Earth was too big and its resources too abundant for humans to cause irreversible harm. There are now around 6.5 billion of us, and virtually no ecosystem has escaped our footprint. But, we have no place else to

true—if conservation is essentially trying to reverse and remove humanity's impact—then this mindset may be at odds with most Christian creation care programs. Many of these programs fundamentally assume that humanity enjoys a place of prominence in the created order. Why? Because Gen 1–2 informs us that we are not only divine image bearers, but the creation of humanity represents the apex of God's creative action.

Michelangelo's *The Creation of Adam* from the Sistine Chapel.

And when these realizations are coupled with the mandate of responsible "dominion" over creation and harmony with creation (Gen 1:26–28), Christian creation care programs see humanity as having an integral, perhaps even managing, role to play. The father and son team of Douglas and Jonathan Moo exemplify this position in their *Creation Care: A Biblical Theology of the Natural World*: "The Bible makes clear that we humans have a unique place in God's creation, the only creatures made 'in the image of God.'"[11] So, "We must ask about the place of humans in 'creation care.'"[12] Their answer? Stewardship, despite the controversy in defining the

---

"move on." Fortunately, there is action to undo some of the damage humans have wrought on the planet. This is the movement known as ecological restoration.

McConnell and Abel, *Environmental Issues*, 327; emphasis original.

11. Moo and Moo, *Creation Care*, 25.
12. Moo and Moo, *Creation Care*, 180.

concept. In their minds, proper stewardship is not indicative of a distant or disconnected persona but rather a deeply connected and vested one. In their minds, the stewardship concept is "conditioned" by the message of Gen 1 in particular and the entire Bible generally:

> But even more important in elaborating the nature and extent of the dominion mandate is the accountability side of the stewardship metaphor. As stewards of creation, human beings must please creation's "owner," the Lord God, in the way they carry out their responsibility. The many biblical assertions about the worth of the created world itself thus set implicit parameters for the exercise of dominion. Believers' stewardship must follow the pattern established by Christ himself.[13]

Sandra Richter shares a similar sentiment. According to *Stewards of Eden*, the creation accounts of Genesis clarify that "for humanity to be named a *ṣelem* (image) is for humanity to be identified as the animate representation of God on this planet."[14] Therefore, "humanity plays a critical role in God's blueprint for the flourishing of this majestic ecosphere in which we find ourselves. Yahweh is indeed the ultimate sovereign, but humanity has been created as his representative to serve as custodian and steward, enacting the Creator's will by living our lives as *a reflection of God's image*."[15]

There, on that beach, it hit me. This popular Christian position—that humanity has a central role to play in the preservation of the environment because of their privileged place in creation—has to be one reason why some scientists continue to believe that Christians, by and large, are ideologically retarded. Christians, at least many of those who are not Young Earth creationists, accept that the earth existed and developed prior to humanity's appearance. And many Christians, regardless of their acceptance or rejection of Young Earth creationism, accept that humanity has played a massive part in the degradation of the world and that the world is

---

13. Moo and Moo, *Creation Care*, 184.
14. Richter, *Stewards of Eden*, 9.
15. Richter, *Stewards of Eden*, 11; emphasis original.

currently far away from its original or intended state. Consequently, these Christians also emphasize that it is humanity who is responsible for the fixing and subsequent maintenance of the created order. So, in adding all this together, many Christians see creation care as an integral element within a larger plan of cosmic redemption that boasts humanity as a featured agent. It is with this last step that the potential disconnect between humanity's role in the ecological conversation appears, and I don't think it gets enough attention.

But was Ben correct? Do most scientists engage ecological conversations with the assumption that humanity's activity ultimately should be restricted in some way? Is it really about having humanity "get out of the way?" Moo and Moo describe a related position which removes any privilege from humanity as a "radical" position.[16] Quoting Edward Abbey, who famously stated that he would rather kill a human than a snake, Moo and Moo state that such an anti-human speciesism is a minority view. Thus,

> it must be acknowledged that few people, including environmentalists, go this far in advocating for complete equality between human beings and other animals. Quite apart from any Christian, religious, or philosophical considerations, the views seem for most people to be contradicted by reality. The very fact that human beings are responsible for damaging the earth in a way no other species has ever done suggest that humans have, at least, unique power to affect their environment and perhaps—especially given our unique ability to think and reflect on these effects—also unique responsibilities.[17]

Yet in the article "Are Humans Part of Ecosystems?," Oliver Houck suggests that Abbey's opinion may be more widely held when he describes an observable category of ecological pundits unified by their perception of humanity as a virus. According to Houck, these proponents argue that humanity's obsession with progression and expansion has pushed the world to its breaking point.[18] Therefore,

---

16. Moo and Moo, *Creation Care*, 181.
17. Moo and Moo, *Creation Care*, 181.
18. Houck, "Are Humans Part of Ecosystems?," 3–4.

for creation to be cared for in a way that will facilitate healing, humans need to radically alter their ethics at best or, at worst, get out of the way.

So, I don't think that Ben's statement was completely off base. Clearly, there are many people who engage the debate of humanity, creation care, and ecology with a profoundly skeptical view regarding the role humanity should play. But even in less antagonistic examples, the role of humanity remains vague. Consider Aldo Leopold's description of a land ethic: "A land ethic reflects the existence of ecological consciousness, and this in turn reflects a conviction of individual responsibility for the health of the land. *Health is the capacity of the land for self-renewal.* Conservation is our effort to understand and preserve this capacity."[19] According to Leopold, whatever humanity's role may be,[20] the emphasis upon self-renewal implies that it will ultimately yield to the land. However, on the whole, the debate is clearly more complicated than what I understood Ben to be saying. This has been put beyond question by several large-scale works, such as McDonnell and Pickett's *Humans as Components of Ecosystems* as well as *The Structure and Dynamics of Human Ecosystems* by Burch, Machlis, and Force. Yet, for Christians, this debate is fundamentally impacted by our sacred texts, which is a variable that is not valued by all participants in the conversation. We are compelled to incorporate Gen 1–2 with its particular emphasis upon the dominion allocated to humanity as well as humanity's relationship with the surrounding ecosystems. So, one must ask, "What is being communicated in these texts? What does the idea of dominion actually communicate? And how does the message of those texts affect the conversation, even with respect to others that do not hold to the same ideological convictions?"

I will admit straight away that I am not trying to persuade anyone of my current positions. I am not trying to systematically

---

19. Leopold, *Sand County Almanac*, 221; emphasis mine.

20. Leopold seems to struggle with this in the paragraphs that follow when he describes dissensions within conservationists. Leopold, *Sand County Almanac*, 221–23.

engage the arguments of Young Earth creationists, proponents of theistic evolution, or anyone else. Nor do I intend to specifically detail the history of the debate regarding Christian theology, creation, and ecology. There are too many nuances, voices, and elements to survey. Besides, such endeavors would go against the objectives of this work. Rather, I hope to offer some musings—reflections and thoughts—about my family's experiences on the Galápagos Islands somewhat jovially as an inroad to a conversation that remains very difficult. If anything, I am convinced there are no easy answers here. Discussions of theology, creation, and ecology are incredibly sophisticated in their own rights. For example, it remains difficult to even come up with a precise definition of ecology.[21] Moreover, go no further than the Zondervan Counterpoints series, in which the volumes *Three Views on Creation and Evolution*[22] and *Four Views on the Historical Adam*[23] feature, to see the complexity of the topics at hand. This means, then, that any conversation that merges them has the potential to become exponentially complicated. Indeed, the way forward is through synthesis, but that synthesis will be exponentially difficult. Therefore, if I touch upon elements of Young Earth creationism, theistic evolution, or Christian environmentalism in this work, so be it. Just realize that I'm not going to dwell on it.

In a subsequent chapter, I examine foundational texts for Christians in this conversation, namely Gen 1–11. In doing so, I hope to show that parts of the text are more ambiguous and culturally conditioned than what most evangelical Christians care to admit. Moreover, I dwell upon another important locus: the place of humanity in the created order and what that may mean.

21. Consider the opening statements of Robert Leo Smith:

> Ecology, *difficult to define precisely*, is the study of the interrelationship of organisms with their total environment, physical and biological. . . . As its various disciplines expand, ecology is being fragmented into specialties with a growing lack of communication between them.

Smith, *Ecology and Field Biology*, 12–13; emphasis mine. Also, Elliott-Graves elaborates on these difficulties in "Ecology."

22. Nelson et al., *Three Views*.

23. Lamoureux et. al., *Four Views*.

The Difficulty of Travel and Humanity

Another chapter continues certain elements established in these opening chapters by detailing the hostilities between humanity and the larger created order. By bringing together texts from the Bible and experiences on the Galápagos Islands, the problems between humanity and the created order are hopefully clarified. The following chapters use the same method, although these chapters rely more on personal experiences rather than textual evidence. The overarching point of all these chapters, however, is that the dynamics of ecological conversations betray a collision of ideals and reality. I conclude with some musings that may (hopefully) impact the conversation moving forward. However, before we do any of this, let's get accustomed to the islands.

2

The Islands Born of Fire

APPROXIMATELY SIX HUNDRED MILES off the west coast of Ecuador, in total isolation, lies a series of volcanic islands that not only continue to dominate biological research but also remain on the bucket list of virtually every world traveler. Sure, six hundred miles may not seem like much to the modern traveler who has been spoiled by Boeing and Airbus, but to people like Charles Darwin, who traveled there in modest wooden ships in the pre-industrial world, the trip there would have seemed like a lifetime, not to mention dangerous. The Pacific Ocean is a treacherous place, and if the conditions are right, it will break ships in half. Nevertheless, the allure is real. Because it is completely isolated, any life that you encounter there feels mystical, as if it was imagined by either the most creative of minds or those tripping on psychedelics. There, birds have blue and pink feet. Tortoises the size of small calves roam the countryside. Green sea turtles the size of kitchen tables float just offshore in the most brilliant of blue water. Penguins swim through bays alongside hammerhead sharks in eighty-five-degree weather. And, if you're lucky, you can experience the volcanic processes that gave birth to the islands millions of years ago.

The Galápagos Island are often described as islands "born of fire" because volcanic hot spots form this archipelago as the

Nazca (tectonic) Plate drifts south and eastward toward the South American plate.

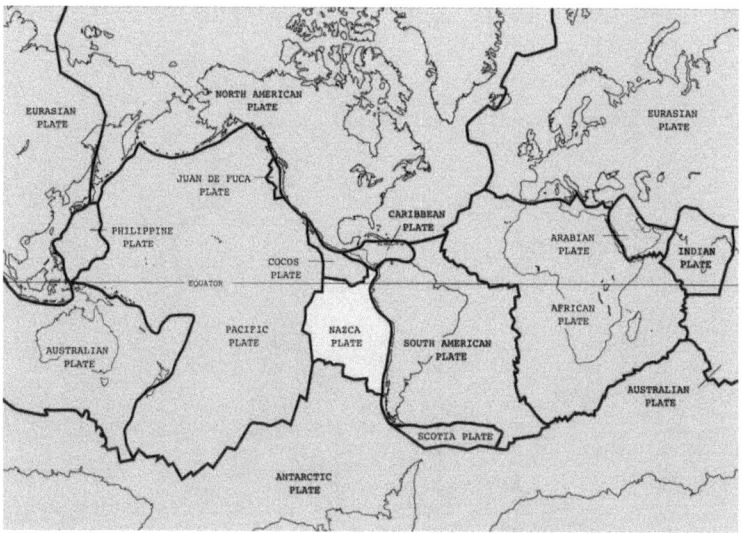

Notice the present tense in this statement. This is because, to be precise, the Galápagos Islands continue to be formed to this day. The Nazca Plate continues to move, and as it does, magma rises and forms new landmasses or adds to already existing ones. Thus, the oldest of the islands are the ones further south and east in the chain, such as Española, San Cristóbal, and Floreana, but the youngest happen to be Isabela and Fernandina, inlands toward the northern and western end of the chain. But the Galápagos Islands could also be described as islands "beholden to ocean currents." During the first quarter of the calendar year, equatorial currents carry warm water toward the island chain producing a warm and rainy season. However, during the third quarter of the year, the Humboldt Current overruns those warm currents to bring cold water and drier air up from Antarctica. As we will discuss later, this shift is critical to the Galápagos ecosystem.

Frigatebirds, Sea Lions, and Darwin

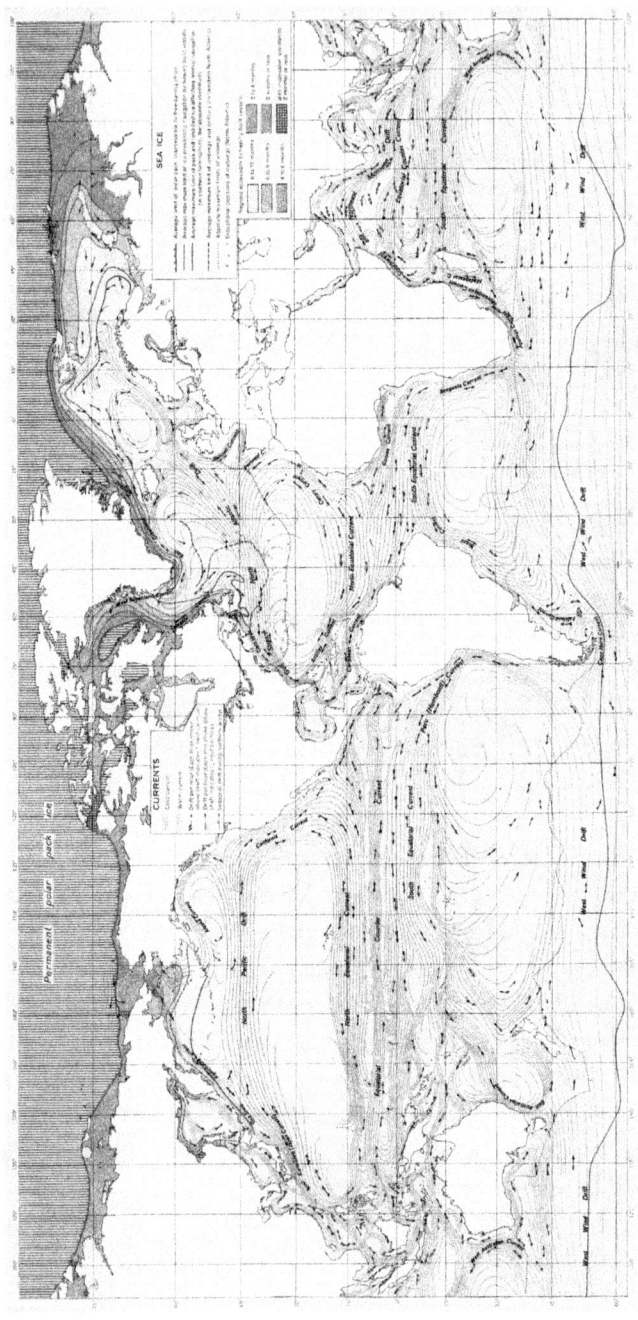

The Islands Born of Fire

What may be something of a surprise, Charles Darwin and the crew of the HMS Beagle did not discover the Galápagos Islands. Various archaeological sites have uncovered evidence of prehistoric occupation, possibly related to fishing, a reality that continues to define the Galápagos way of life to this day. Yet, the archipelago's modern history begins in the sixteenth century with the Spanish Empire. Tomas de Berlanga, a Spanish bishop, is often credited with the modern discovery of the islands when his ship was violently blown off-course in his attempt to navigate to Peru. Yet the most nostalgic era of occupation happened during the golden age of piracy, when pirates made extensive use of the islands as a haven and depot for their stolen loot. As stated by Oxford and Watkins, "The islands were strategically convenient for pirates because they were sufficiently distant from the mainland to permit escape, yet close enough to trade routes and coastal cities for raids."[1] More legitimately, whalers, fishermen, and other merchants came to populate the islands in hopes of turning a profit off the backs of the diverse animal resources. In fact, whalers as far as Nantucket were reportedly drawn to the islands. Because the archipelago is a breeding ground for various species of whales, it became a lucrative locus for biological commodities like whale oil and baleen, the latter of which was used in whips, springs, hoop frames for skirts, corsets, and umbrellas.[2] In fact, the Galápagos Islands remained "the Pacific base for whalers" until the nineteenth century, when it shifted to the vicinity of Japan.[3] However, there was a darker side to these economic possibilities. These endeavors also decimated certain indigenous animal populations, such as the tortoises and sea lions. In fact, certain populations were hunted to extinction. Most heinously, this trend continued into the twentieth century as the economic possibilities associated with the tuna industry encouraged overfishing and questionable harvesting practices.[4]

---

1. Oxford and Watkins, *Galápagos*, 9.
2. Oxford and Watkins, *Galápagos*, 10.
3. Oxford and Watkins, *Galápagos*, 10.
4. Oxford and Watkins, *Galápagos*, 12.

Frigatebirds, Sea Lions, and Darwin

Ecuador gained independence from Spain in 1832. When this happened, the newly declared nation annexed the islands as their own. Yet, particularly due to its distance from the mainland, the immediate question was what to do with these newly acquired landmasses. History had shown through the previous centuries that any settlement was extremely difficult due to the harsh ecological conditions. Whether they were pirates or whalers, any settlement has proven to be extremely precarious. The decision then was to implement a program of colonization that utilized social outcasts of various kinds, public dissidents, and shady businesses. The logic must have been rooted in a low-risk philosophy. If the colonies failed, not much would be lost. However, if they somehow succeeded, the infrastructure for more lucrative and promising settlements would piggyback off the grunt work of their society's most vulnerable.

One of those colonization efforts was linked with El Progresso. This agricultural center was started on San Cristóbal by the ruthless Manuel Cobos. It originally served the oil and tannery businesses, but it also functioned alongside sugar plantations utilizing convict labor. By all accounts, the atmosphere was appalling and dangerous. Nevertheless, it was enough to establish San Cristóbal and Puerto Baquerizo Moreno as the political capital of the islands. It's still that way today.

Yet El Progresso was not the only problematic settlement. Probably the most famous was the prison colony that populated the island of Isabela during and around the conclusion of World War II. Then-President Jose Maria Velasco Ibarra determined that Isabela was to be the outlet for an overcrowded prison population. What's more, there was a glut of material and resources left over by the Americans in the wake of World War II because they had used it as an outpost in the Pacific. So, when Ibarra added these two realities together, he created a penal colony with hard labor and the reinforcement of the island's infrastructure embedded in its settlement philosophy. Predictably, a copious number of inmates died over the colony's thirteen-year existence due to extreme work environments. Inmates ultimately rebelled, escaped, and hijacked a yacht, a series of events that apparently ushered in the colony's closure.

The last remaining vestiges of that penal colony can be seen at what's called the "Wall of Tears" (El Muro de las Lagrimas). It's a twenty-five-foot-high wall of lava rock that was systematically built and rebuilt over many years, and its function was apparently completely punitive. It served no purpose but to occupy the prisoners' focus and channel all their energy to non-seditious activity. It still exists today at the end of a lengthy bike path, completely isolated from any settlement. And when we visited there in 2024, I experienced the tears that this wall could elicit.

We were staying at the La Laguna Hotel right across from the Poza de los Flamingos, and one morning, we decided to rent bikes and head up the bike path toward the wall. Admittedly, it was hot, and the air was stagnant, and when you go into the interior of Isabela the humidity increases as well. Consequently, when these factors combined with the overall fatigue and steady uphill climb of the twelve-kilometer path, two of my three kids became emotionally overwhelmed when they were confronted by the hike at the end of the path. Said hike eventually took you to one of the highest points in Isabela, producing a breathtaking view of Puerto Villamil, the Pacific Ocean, and Isabela's Sierra Negra Volcano. Yet on that day, the beauty didn't matter. Instead, my children cried tears of solidarity with so many before them.

Frigatebirds, Sea Lions, and Darwin

The Wall of Tears in Isabela.

But without a doubt, animal life, terrestrial and marine, is what defines the Galápagos Islands. Sure, these islands were immortalized by Darwin and his evolutionary ideas, but the perpetual beauty and overwhelming biodiversity and endemism of the islands entrench its status as one of the most desirable places on earth. And yes, it would overwhelm anyone to try and catalog all the species currently living in the Galápagos ecosystem. Yet what is amazing, but easier to process, is the simple fact that the Galápagos Islands boasts the highest level of endemic species vis-à-vis any other place on earth. Thirty percent of all plant species are endemic to the island chain. Twenty percent of animals are endemic. And most famous of those are the Galápagos tortoise, the marine iguana, and the Galápagos penguin. Other famous animals include various species of boobies, the so-called Darwin finches, hammerhead sharks, whale sharks, and Galápagos sea lions. Yet, as fascinating as this catalog of animals is, invertebrates account for the highest population of diversity within the Galápagos ecosystem

The Islands Born of Fire

(as is the case with all ecosystems). Some estimates posit that invertebrates account for fifty percent of the total biodiversity. These barely visible creatures have the greatest impact on the ecosystem. Whether as pollinators, active participants in organic recycling, or merely as part of the food chain, without them, the ecosystem couldn't function efficiently.

However, all this biodiversity exists on a knife's edge. It's a fragile system that is highly susceptible to the introduction of species.[5] According to one statistic, seventy-five percent of the world's recorded extinctions of flora and fauna have occurred on the Galápagos Islands, and of those, eighty-five percent have been linked to invasive species. By some estimations, over one hundred eighty species on the Galápagos Islands are in danger of extinction. Yet, as a ray of hope, the Galápagos Islands is also home to some massive restoration projects, the most famous of which is undoubtedly the restoration of the Galápagos tortoises. It's a story of perseverance, disappointment, good fortune, genetic engineering, and a single tortoise named Lonesome George.

The Galápagos Islands has been home to fifteen different tortoise species throughout its history. Considered a "keystone species" as well as an "ecosystem engineer," they "structure the ecology of the islands as they plod up and down volcanic hillsides, munching on grasses and fruits and depositing seeds along the way."[6] Most importantly, they have come to represent and symbolize the Galápagos and its conservation efforts more than any other of its endemic species. "It is the giant tortoises who are the most telling mascots of the archipelago's conservation history."[7] However, they became such a symbol only because of the hole from which they have been rescued. In short, they were essentially brought to extinction by human activity during the nineteenth century. In fact, three of the fifteen species exist now only in historical memory.

---

5. Data in the paragraph is summarized from Galápagos Conservation Trust, "Global Relevance." Even if exact percentages are debated, they represent the delicate nature and vulnerability of the ecosystem.

6. Hennessy, *On the Backs of Tortoises*, 3.

7. Hennessy, *On the Backs of Tortoises*, 6.

Yet, against all odds, today they are bouncing back thanks to an aggressive conservation program that continues to feed off the memory of Lonesome George.

George was a tortoise found on the island of Pinta in 1971. What was shocking about George was that up to that point, conservationists thought that his species (*Chelonoidis abingdoni*) had been eradicated from the island. So, what did they do when they found him? They put him in a box and shipped him to Santa Cruz with the intention of using him as a breeder for a rejuvenation project. Unfortunately, there was no female of his species found, not just in the archipelago but anywhere in the world. A $10,000 reward was even floated to inspire people and zoos to look harder. But alas, all was for nothing. So, the keepers of Lonesome George pivoted. They brought in related, but different, species with the hope that he would provide a hybrid heir. But this too would not work. Even after altering his diet, among other things, George would not mate with any females brought to him. He apparently just carried on without any interest, stubbornly refusing to procreate.[8] Then it happened. In June 2012, Lonesome George died, and so too did *Chelonoidis abingdoni* with him.

Yet, biologists had already been getting creative in their conservation efforts before George died. Members of an expedition to the Wolf Volcano on Isabela in 2008 chose to look more closely at peculiar structural features on the shells of a distinct tortoise population. Instead of the more pronounced dome-shaped shells, several tortoises exhibited a smaller, more saddleback shape. Upon analyzing the blood samples, researchers found them to be hybrids, a cross between the native species of Isabela and other islands, including Floreana and Pinta.[9] Consequently, researchers implemented another resurrection plan that essentially ran concurrently with the plan constructed around Lonesome George. Researchers attempted to determine if there was enough viable DNA in the hybrid tortoises from Isabela to resurrect the extinct species from Pinta and Floreana, or perhaps to mate with George. Sadly, for George, this did not prove successful. So, in 2015, researchers went back to the area around the Wolf Volcano on northern Isabela to transplant a core of these hybrids back to a breeding center for a more controlled environment to facilitate the resurrection of the Floreana and Pinta species.

If you are reading this and you're beginning to realize the role genetics and human agency will have in conservation, you're spot on. They have essentially become two sides of the same coin. For example, efforts surrounding the sustainability of the tortoise species currently revolve around different man-made breeding centers throughout the archipelago, which are designed to lay and fertilize

---

8. This is, admittedly, an oversimplification. Biologists and conservationists consistently struggled with George's inability to procreate, culminating in two instances where he failed to fertilize a batch of eggs laid by female tortoises living with him. After his death, a necropsy revealed "an anatomical deformity," demonstrating that George was incapable of mating rather than just not being interested in it. For an account of these struggles, see Hennessy, *On the Backs of Tortoises*, 161–63.

9. How did this happen? People point to sea merchants and pirates who made use of the islands early on in its modern history. For many reasons, tortoises were thrown overboard near these islands only to float ashore and resume living.

eggs, hatch them, and then raise the baby tortoises until about five years of age. In short, the breeding centers seek to control a very complex process to secure a high degree of success.

But why wait five years to release them into the wild, you may ask? The mortality rate of baby tortoises, due to predators and a lack of resources, remains rather high until about five years of age. In other words, scientists wait five years to control the processes more effectively and optimize success. Yet, as shown by the tortoise population, conservation may also involve the resurrecting of species, which adds another layer to an already complex endeavor. In other words, conservation is not just about controlling the breeding of populations. Rather, it's also about utilizing cutting-edge genetic analyses to ensure a certain level of genetic diversity alongside genetic continuity to optimize success in the resurrection and reintroduction of species. As shown by Miller and company, researchers subject potential breeders to a variety of genetic texts and simulations to determine which pool of applicants have the highest potential.[10]

In addition to the work being done with the Galápagos tortoises, there is a massive undertaking to restore the ecosystem on Floreana in the wake of the invasive feline, rat, cow, and goat populations.[11] On the one hand, the invasive populations must be eradicated. On the other hand, extant species must be protected at the same time that extinct species are reintroduced. And such reintroduction is only possible because the extinct species, like the Floreana mockingbird and Galápagos racer, exist on other islands. Additionally, land iguanas are being reintroduced on Santiago, and the woodpecker finch is making a comeback on Pinzon Island. In fact, what is being observed on Pinzon is another modern-day success story. Once the rats were eradicated there, the Galápagos rail and the cactus finch were free to naturally repopulate the island. Even the Galápagos tortoise has settled on Pinzon as its natural reproduction has been recorded.

10. Miller et. al., "Genetic Pedigree," 620–30.
11. Galápagos Conservation Trust, "Floreana."

The Islands Born of Fire

Forgive me, but I could go on and one. All of this testifies to the uniqueness of the Galápagos Islands. Its allure is captivating to those who love to travel and/or observe wildlife, and it consumes copious amounts of money and political clout to ensure its survival as one of the most idealistic places on earth. And for our purposes here, its allure and surreal quality are the stimuli that have propelled the following musings.

3

Social Media, Genesis, and Intentions

WE LIVE IN AN information age. More than any other moment of human history, information is at our fingertips. Whether on our computers or our smartphones, virtually any type of information is only a few clicks or mere seconds away. This is a good and bad thing. For example, recently it was Ginny's birthday, and one day prior, she looked at me and said, "Am I going to have a birthday cake?" I stared at her blankly, going through several scenarios in my head. There was a Dollar General down the street, and so I could go there and look for cake and icing mix. However, these thoughts were interrupted by another thought, particularly because the desire was not to spend any money. Could I just make the cake from scratch? For a short while, I considered how I was going to pull this off, but then I got an idea: I would look up a recipe for cake and icing on the Internet.

I am pleased to report that while my family enjoyed the next afternoon frolicking with friends at a private pool, I intertwined my daily work responsibilities with making a cake (with icing, mind you) from scratch. And that night, my efforts found the appropriate response: everyone thought it was a good cake . . . no, an "excellent cake." Crisis averted.

In other instances, the Internet has taught me how to fix my automatic garage door, replace faucet cartridges, figure out what my oldest daughter put her foot through one afternoon while practicing soccer in the backyard (it was a distribution box for our septic tank system), and a host of other responsibilities associated with homeownership. However, there's a downside to the amount of information and the ease at which we get it. With so much information out there, what's useful and what's useless? What's truthful, and what's there to misinform?

As I write this, it's the very end of 2024, and the residue of the extensive disinformation campaigns that plagued the 2016 and 2020 United States presidential races are still a lightning rod for controversy, particularly since Donald Trump has recently been reelected as president. More recently, the Russian/Ukrainian and Israeli/Hamas-Hezbollah conflicts boast active fronts on social media where propaganda and disinformation are disseminated with great effect. But without a doubt, what makes this so maddening is that the context whence so much questionable information comes is also the context where people fight to establish the credibility of that information. In other words, questionable information is disseminated on various digital platforms, and it's often on those same platforms where people try to determine what is legitimate and illegitimate information. It's a mess.

Consequently, it goes without saying that our information age is a double-edged sword, and social media platforms, such as Twitter, Facebook, TikTok, Bluesky, and more, have become theaters of an ideological and culture war. In my lifetime, I have watched these platforms come to fruition, functioning to spread useless (but innocuous) personal information only to then develop into soapboxes where people feel free to caricature, create straw man arguments, trade insults over differences, and create echo-chambers. The result is digital quicksand where those who fall in may be buried as their efforts to escape ultimately secure their intellectual demise. Efforts presumed to be helpful are actually counterproductive.

Frigatebirds, Sea Lions, and Darwin

One person who makes great use of social media platforms for the dissemination of his ideas is Ken Ham. He is the founder of the widely influential Answers in Genesis, which started out as Creation Science Ministries but was rebranded as Answers in Genesis in 1997.[1] It is an "apologetic ministry dedicated to helping Christians defend their faith and proclaim the good news of Jesus Christ effectively."[2] More specifically, it focuses "on providing answers to questions about the Bible—particularly the book of Genesis—regarding key issues such as creation, evolution, science, and the age of the earth."[3] Ham is most famous for two biblically based theme-park-like attractions, both of which are just up the interstate from where I live in Kentucky: the Creation Museum and the Ark Encounter. A radio host and a TV personality, Ham is also an avid blogger and social media user, all of which function as vehicles for arguing his theological and ideological points.

Admittedly, he's very effective in what he attempts to do. Having approximately one hundred thousand followers on Twitter and several hundred thousand on Facebook, he not only supports the positions of like-minded people with fodder for discussion but also engages in online debates with his detractors through a modus operandi that highlights what he believes to be fallacies and inconsistencies among his opponent's arguments. For example, consider this very lengthy tweet made by Ham on June 12, 2023.

---

1. Ham, "History."
2. Ham, "About."
3. Ham, "About."

Social Media, Genesis, and Intentions

← Post

Ken Ham ✓
@aigkenham

Who should you trust first? God or the scientist? God or the Christian academic?

Many times over the years, I've had a number of conversations with Christians who won't accept the days of creation as ordinary days and vehemently defend millions of years and other evolutionary beliefs. Often, the person talking to me has quoted various Christian academics, well known theologians/Christian leaders, or certain church fathers claiming that I should give up my literal Genesis position because these academics/famous Christians do not agree with me.

My answer to them has been "but what does God clearly state in His Word. I judge the people you quoted against God's Word, not the other way round."

I have certainly been scoffed at and mocked at over the years because of my position. Now don't get me wrong, I respect scholarship. But regardless, we need to recognize that we could have 100 Ph.D's from Harvard university, but compared to what God's knows we would still know nearly nothing.

When I teach children about dinosaurs, creation and evolution, I like to ask them these questions:

"Has any human being always been there?" They answer, "no."
"Has any scientist always been there?" They answer, "no."
"Does any human being know everything?" They answer, "no."
"Does any scientist know everything?" They answer, "no."
"Who is the only one who has always been there?" They shout out, "God."
"Who is the only one who knows everything?" The shout out, "God."

I then ask:

"Who is the one we should always trust first? God or the scientist?" They call out "God."

← Post

"Who is the one we should always trust first? God or the scientist?" They call out "God."

And I could add, "Who should we always trust first, God, the scientist, the theologian, the teacher, the pastor, the professor?" And the answer will always be "God."

In a way that sounds rather simplistic. In fact, I've had people who oppose my position claim that I have too simplistic a belief to just take Genesis 1–11 as it is written. Now when someone claims it's too simplistic, I believe this is showing up a problem we all have to battle with because it's a part of our nature, the sin nature we have, because we are descendants of Adam. The problem is pride.

God's Word has a lot to say about pride:

"When pride comes, then comes disgrace, but with the humble is wisdom." (Proverbs 11:2).

"Do you see a man who is wise in his own eyes? There is more hope for a fool than for him" (Proverbs 26:12).

And God's Word tells how to gain wisdom and knowledge:

"The fear of the LORD is the beginning of knowledge" (Proverbs 1:7).
"The fear of the LORD is the beginning of wisdom" (Proverbs 9:10).

I would rather stand before the Lord and say that I'm guilty of simplistically believing what His Word states in Genesis than to trust the word of fallible humans and reinterpret God's Word.

I'm reminded about this so called "simplistic" approach when I read what Jesus said about children:

"'Truly, I say to you, unless you turn and become like children, you will never enter the kingdom of heaven. Whoever humbles himself like this child is the greatest in the kingdom of heaven.'" (Matthew 18:3–4)."

← Post

"'Truly, I say to you, unless you turn and become like children, you will never enter the kingdom of heaven. Whoever humbles himself like this child is the greatest in the kingdom of heaven.'" (Matthew 18:3–4)."

It is so much easier for children who have not had years of indoctrination from the world to believe God's Word as written. Reading Genesis for them is just like reading a history book. Well, it is history, and history as God had it recorded for us. Sadly, the more educated people come, many find it harder to believe God's Word as written in Genesis. And it's not because Genesis is literal history, but I believe it's because of pride.

And a reason for that is we all have an underlying problem.

It doesn't matter who we are, we all have sinful hearts.

"For all have sinned and fall short of the glory of God." (Romans 3:23).

The origin of sin is found in Genesis 3 when Adam and Eve were tempted by the devil to disobey God. Now consider two elements of the temptation that help us understand our sin nature:

Genesis 3:1: "He said to the woman, "Did God actually say...""

Note the first attack by the devil was on the Word of God to get Adam and Eve to doubt God's Word so that doubt would lead to unbelief.

Genesis 3:5: "For God knows that when you eat of it your eyes will be opened, and you will be like God, knowing good and evil."

The second part of the temptation was really to offer them to be their own god.

We know Adam took the fruit and disobeyed God and brought sin and the judgment of death into the world. God's Word states:

33

← Post

We know that Adam took the fruit and disobeyed God and brought sin and the judgment of death into the world. God's Word states:

"Therefore, just as sin came into the world through one man, and death through sin, and so death spread to all men because all sinned—for sin indeed was in the world before the law was given, but sin is not counted where there is no law. Yet death reigned from Adam to Moses, even over those whose sinning was not like the transgression of Adam, who was a type of the one who was to come" (Romans 5:12–14).

So we have that sin nature. And Genesis 3:1 and 3:5 sum up that nature:

Our propensity will be to doubt the Word of God, as we would rather trust the word of man. I see that over and over again with Christian leaders/academics who would rather trust man's word (beliefs) about millions of years and evolution instead of God's Word as it's clearly stated in Genesis 1–11.

Also, we have this propensity to be our own god. We want to decide truth for ourselves. We see ourselves as being proud of what we know. We think we can reason correctly by ourselves and so we have that problem of intellectual pride wanting intellectual respectability.

I believe this is why there is so much compromise in the church when it comes to God's Word in Genesis. Our heart is such that we would rather trust man's word that God's Word, and so we have a problem with intellectual pride and thus we cave to peer pressure. We must guard against this. However, none of us like being called anti-intellectual, or anti-academic. And we will be called that if we believe in six literal days of creation and a young earth and universe.

But I often think about those in Hebrews 11 and the Christian martyrs of the past. They were sawn in half, thrown to lions, burned alive, lived in caves, were destitute and suffered many atrocities. And yet, so many Christians today cave because they are belittled by secular academics for believing the "simplistic" account of creation, Fall, Flood and Tower of Babel as related in Scripture.

I wonder how many in the church today would have stood with

← Post

I wonder how many in the church today would have stood with Shadrach, Meshach, and Abednego. Would you? Who do you trust first, God or the scientist?

"'Now if you are ready when you hear the sound of the horn, pipe, lyre, trigon, harp, bagpipe, and every kind of music, to fall down and worship the image that I have made, well and good. But if you do not worship, you shall immediately be cast into a burning fiery furnace. And who is the god who will deliver you out of my hands?' Shadrach, Meshach, and Abednego answered and said to the king, 'O Nebuchadnezzar, we have no need to answer you in this matter. If this be so, our God whom we serve is able to deliver us from the burning fiery furnace, and He will deliver us out of your hand, O king. But if not, be it known to you, O king, that we will not serve your gods or worship the golden image that you have set up.'" (Daniel 3:15–18)

7:17 AM Jun 12, 2023 · **23K** Views

○ 37   ⇅ 64   ♡ 279   ⬜ 17   ↑↓

Below is a transcript of this posting.

Who should you trust first? God or the scientist? God or the theologian? God or the Christian academic?

Many times over the years, I've had a number of conversations with Christians who won't accept the days of creation as ordinary days and vehemently defend millions of years and other evolutionary beliefs. Often, the person talking to me has quoted various Christian academics, well known [sic] theologians/Christian leaders, or certain church fathers claiming that I should give up my literal Genesis position because these academics/famous Christians do not agree with me.

My answer to them has been "but what does God clearly state in His Word. I judge the people you quoted against God's Word, not the other way round."

I have certainly been scoffed at and mocked at over the years because of my position. Now don't get me wrong. I respect scholarship. But regardless, we need to recognize that we could have 100 Ph.D.'s from Harvard university, but compared to what God's [sic] knows we would still know nearly nothing.

When I teach children about dinosaurs, creation and evolution, I like to ask them these questions:

"Has any human being always been there?" They answer, "no."

"Has any scientist always been there?" They answer, "no."

"Does any human being know everything?" They answer, "no" [sic]

"Does any scientist know everything?" They answer, "no."

"Who is the only one who has always been there?" They shout out, "God."

"Who is the only one who knows everything?" The [sic] shout out, "God."

I then ask:

"Who is the one we should always trust first? God or the scientist?" They call out "God."

And I could add, "Who should we always trust first, God, the scientist, the theologian, the teacher, the pastor, the professor?" And the answer will always be "God."

In a way that sounds rather simplistic. In fact, I've had people who oppose my position claim that I have too simplistic a belief to just take Genesis 1–11 as it is written. Now when someone claims it's too simplistic, I believe this is showing us a problem we all have to battle with because it's a part of our nature, the sin nature we have, because we are descendants of Adam. The problem is pride.

God's Word has a lot to say about pride:

"When pride comes, then comes disgrace, but with the humble is wisdom" (Proverbs 11:2).

"Do you see a man who is wise in his own eyes? There is more hope for a fool than for him" (Proverbs 26:12).

And God's Word tells how to gain wisdom and knowledge:

"The fear of the LORD is the beginning of knowledge" (Proverbs 1:7).

"The fear of the LORD is the beginning of wisdom" (Proverbs 9:10).

I would rather stand before the Lord and say that I'm guilty of simplistically believing what His Word states in Genesis than to trust the word of fallible humans and reinterpret God's Word.

I'm reminded about this so called [sic] "simplistic" approach when I read what Jesus said about children:

"Truly, I say to you, unless you turn and become like children, you will never enter the kingdom of heaven. Whoever humbles himself like this child is the greatest in the kingdom of heaven" (Matthew 18:3–4).

It is so much easier for children who have not had years of indoctrination from the world to believe God's Word as written. Reading Genesis for them is just like reading a history book. Well, it is history, and history as God had it recorded for us. Sadly, the more educated people become, many find it harder to believe God's Word as written in Genesis. And it's not because Genesis is literal history, but I believe it's because of pride.

And a reason for that is we all have an underlying problem.

It doesn't matter who we are, we all have sinful hearts.

"For all have sinned and fall short of the glory of God," (Romans 3:23).

The origin of sin is found in Genesis 3 when Adam and Eve were tempted by the devil to disobey God. Now consider two elements of the temptation that help us understand our sin nature:

Genesis 3:1: "He said to the woman, 'Did God actually say . . .'"

Note the first attack by the devil was on the Word of God to get Adam and Eve to doubt God's Word so that doubt would lead to unbelief.

Genesis 3:5: "For God knows that when you eat of it your eyes will be opened, and you will be like God, knowing good and evil."

The second part of the temptation was really to offer them to be their own god.

We know Adam took the fruit and disobeyed God and brought sin and the judgment of death into the world. God's Word states:

"Therefore, just as sin came into the world through one man, and death through sin, and so death spread to all men because all sinned—for sin indeed was in the world before the law was given, but sin is not counted where there is no law. Yet death reigned from Adam to Moses, even over those whose sinning was not like the transgression of Adam, who was a type of the one who was to come" (Romans 5:12–14).

So we have that sin nature. And Genesis 3:1 and 3:5 sum up that nature:

Our propensity will be to doubt the Word of God, as we would rather trust the word of man. I see that over and over again with Christian leaders/academics who would rather trust man's word (beliefs) about millions of years and evolution instead of God's Word as it's clearly stated in Genesis 1–11.

Also, we have this propensity to be our own god. We want to decide truth for ourselves. We see ourselves as being proud of what we know. We think we can reason correctly by ourselves and so we have that problem of intellectual pride wanting intellectual respectability.

I believe this is why there is so much compromise in the church when it comes to God's Word in Genesis. Our heart is such that we would rather trust man's word that God's Word, and so we have a problem with intellectual pride and thus we cave to peer pressure. We must guard against this. However, none of us like being called anti-intellectual, or anti-academic. And we will be called that if we believe in six literal days of creation and a young earth and universe.

But I often think about those in Hebrews 11 and the Christian martyrs of the past. They were sawn in half, thrown to lions, burned alive, lived in caves, were destitute and suffered many atrocities. And yet, so many Christians today cave because they are belittled by secular academics for believing the "simplistic" account of creation, Fall, Flood and Tower of Babel as related in Scripture.

I wonder how many in the church today would have stood with Shadrach, Meshach, and Abednego. Would you? Who do you trust first, God or the scientist?

"Now if you are ready when you hear the sound of the horn, pipe, lyre, trigon, harp, bagpipe, and every kind of music, to fall down and worship the image that I have made, well and good. But if you do not worship, you shall immediately be cast into a burning fiery furnace. And who is the god who will deliver you out of my hands?" Shadrach, Meshach, and Abednego answered and said to the king, "O Nebuchadnezzar, we have no need to answer you in this matter. If this be so, our God whom we serve is able to deliver us from the burning fiery furnace, and he will deliver us out of your hand, O king. But if not, be it known to you, O king, that we will not serve your gods or worship the golden image that you have set up."" [sic] (Daniel 3:15–18)

The first thing that Ham does is create antagonism. Specifically, it's Scripture versus anyone. When it comes to Scripture, people are either against it or want to change it, although terms and categories that he invokes are never precisely defined. What's more, Ham clearly positions himself to be on the side of Scripture, which is foundational to his apologetic. Ham's argumentation is not just a defense of Scripture, it's also a defense of his interpretive conclusions. More importantly, they are two sides of the same coin, and if he is successful in establishing that any differing interpretation is also hostile to Scripture, then he has the upper hand. Of course, this only works with an audience that has a high view of Scripture, but Ham knows his audience.

Ham also always anticipates rebuttals. All good apologists must do so. So, in this post, he anticipates and responds to the accusation that his interpretive conclusions are too simplistic by connecting any dissention toward his positions with pride. He also connects his positions with the teachings of Jesus. According to Ham, his "simple understanding" embodies the humility and childlike faith that Jesus said was necessary to enter the kingdom of God. In the case of the former, Ham rachets up the rhetoric when he joins differing interpretations to pride in general and the fall of humanity and original sin specifically. In other words, Ham is essentially arguing that his interpretive opponents not only succumb to primal urges born at the moment of humanity's great disobedience but also perpetuate the spiritual separation from their Creator. Nevertheless, there's one final step to this argument. Ham positions himself among the great defenders of the faith when he notes a kinship with the names of Heb 11 and Dan 3.

In the end, Ham's arguments are always intense. There is always a lot of posturing and assertions of superiority layered with pietistic claims. Yet, Ham's arguments always strike me as a bit disproportionate. For example, the appeal to Heb 11 and Dan 3 is over the top. The fact is that Ham is arguing for an interpretation of a text in a social context where he will suffer no mortal danger for his positions. This is a stark difference from the imperial contexts assumed by both Daniel and Hebrews. Also, when he states, "I would rather stand before the Lord and say that I'm guilt of simplistically believing what His Word states in Genesis than to trust the word of fallible humans and reinterpret God's Word," he reframes the issue of solving a legitimate interpretive ambiguity as a normative issue, that is, an issue that must be accepted.

I'm sorry, that's too much, and it lacks the sensitivity necessary for what normative issues should be. To put it colloquially, to draw a line in the sand around such a rich, complex, and ambiguous text smacks of a certain naivety that will ultimately do more harm than good, particularly around people who know how to navigate similar texts from the ancient Near East. Nevertheless, I digress.

Ham also seems to enjoy constructing camps into which interpretive conclusions must fall. There are usually at least two camps where one is populated by those on the side of Scripture and the others are populated by those who consider their views to be better than Scripture. In other words, there's a category of those that take Scripture seriously and have a high view of it and there's another populated by those that don't take the Bible seriously (and thus have a low view of Scripture). Yet, critical to determining who populates each camp is Ham's own understanding of the texts, which are always bolstered by claims of "taking the Bible seriously." You can verify this modus operandi by merely perusing through his blogs, social media posts, and other publications.

I confess freely that I received my formal education at schools widely understood to be "conservative." Some would even describe them as fundamentalist. As such, each institution has an expressed commitment to the authority of Scripture as one of their distinctive characteristics that ultimately permeates every objective, initiative, and celebration.[4] To each, Scripture is *the* canon, the measuring stick, for understanding God Almighty, our actions, and our beliefs. In other words, I have been formed by institutions that take the Bible seriously and have a high view of Scripture. Most importantly, I have also adopted these commitments for myself. We certainly understand Scripture to be God's Word. However, at each of these institutions I was also shown what it means for God to have used a particular culture, living in a particular part of the world, at a particular point in world history to communicate his divine revelation to humanity.

After spending approximately two-and-a-half decades at institutions like Indiana Wesleyan University and Asbury Theological Seminary, I am irrevocably entrenched in my conviction that while Scripture is God's word, it's also a text. But more importantly, it's an ancient text. Thus, it's been conditioned by customs and conventions very different from our own. In the mind of John Walton, ancient Israel was part of a cultural river that flowed over and through everything, including their texts.[5] This means that if

---

4. For Asbury Theological Seminary's Statement of Faith, see "Our Statement of Faith." For Indiana Wesleyan's Mission and other defining characteristics, see "University Profile."

5. Walton, *Ancient Near Eastern Thought*, 5–6.

we want to understand the points being made through their texts, we must understand fundamentally the texts of Scripture as an ancient Near Eastern text. In my mind, it's rather straightforward. If you take seriously the notion that God *used* Israel to communicate his divine message of cosmic redemption, and if you want to understand what God is saying, you must understand the literary mechanisms that they would have used.

Therefore, what does this mean for texts like Gen 1–3? What does this mean for the way one employs those texts to form positions about creation, ecology, and humanity's role in all of it? Fundamentally, it means that the intentions of the author through the text are critical. If the words of the Bible were to have any communicative value to the people of ancient Israel, *they* needed to understand its message. Using something that wouldn't have translated into their worldview and conceptual world would have had a limited effect, at best. It would have been nonsense at worst. Rather, efficient communication happens when the message aligns with familiar concepts, conventions, etc.

So, what does this mean for you and me as twenty-first-century Christians? It means that the onus is on us to understand those ancient concepts and mechanisms that are integral to the message.

This point, perhaps more than anything else, convinced me during my formal training that reading similar texts from the ancient world is imperative. I have found that the more that you are exposed to the conventions that defined the composition of literature in ancient Israel's context, the easier it is to identify those conventions in Scripture.[6] And when you can identify those conventions in Scripture, you will be more efficient in identifying Scripture's alignment and deviation from them. This is absolutely critical to the theological points that Scripture is trying to make. Moreover, this also means that reading Scripture comparatively (with similar texts from the ancient world) is not about lowering one's view of Scripture or relegating it to just another ancient text, as if the Bible assumes a position on par with the Gilgamesh Epic

---

6. Christopher Hays discusses this in terms of developing a certain level of cultural literacy. See Hays, *Hidden Riches*.

or the Baal Cycle. It's about gaining an appreciation for Scripture's message as something that fundamentally positions itself as countercultural and even superior to the view of the popular culture.

A Ugaritic Tablet Containing a Portion of the Baal Cycle.

So, what is Gen 1 and beyond saying? Well, to put it bluntly, these chapters are saying a lot. Consider *The Manifold Beauty of Genesis One*, which has been published in recent memory.[7] In this book, Gregg Davidson and Kenneth Turner demonstrate how a singular chapter can say different things based on different considerations. More specifically, they argue that the semantic possibilities of the chapter are realized when the reader recognizes particular

---

7. Davidson and Turner, *Manifold Beauty*.

"layers" that mutually coexist with each other. For example, they refer to one layer as a "song," which is derived from the poetic structure of the chapter. There is also the polemical layer of the text, which emphasizes the theology that subverts many aspects of the prevailing worldview. And there are also layers that highlight the covenantal ideal, creation as a temple, a liturgical framework, and as a symbolic account of Israel's land inheritance, respectively. Ultimately, Davidson and Turner state, "Each reading brings out something that was always true, but only apprehended and appreciated when approached from a different angle.... Each new light—each perspective—yields another layer of theological and artistic beauty."[8]

However, one should not go too far afield. Suggestions that any meaning is possible are nonsensical. Davidson and Turner suggest as much when they say that not all understandings are valid.[9] This means, then, that interpretive boundaries are necessary. If a text means everything, then it really means nothing. Consequently, the question that quickly follows the ideas of Davidson and Turner centers on how one establishes the boundaries of meaning. Admittedly, this is where the assumptions of the reader come into play. For example, if you believe that meaning is largely a reader-oriented phenomenon, then your interpretive endeavors will lead you in a very different direction than those who believe that an author has something to say through the text. As for me, I grew up hearing, in one way or another, that good Christians are supposed to determine what God says to us through the text. Moreover, there was one meaning, and any interpretive method worth its salt helped you find that meaning. One should consider what was said in the text, and one should consider relevant literary and historical issues on the way to obtaining that message. In fact, the latter were critical considerations because they would potentially reveal unstated variables that affected what was intended to be communicated. As for the reader, it was customary to say that their responsibility was to figure out the meaning, not create it. In other words, there was only one meaning, and that meaning was

---

8. Davidson and Turner, *Manifold Beauty*, 172.
9. Davidson and Turner, *Manifold Beauty*, 172.

"right." Other readings were "wrong." Ultimately, it was a relatively black-and-white scenario.

Over time, I have come to realize a few things. First, while I wouldn't trade this foundational instruction for anything, it didn't accommodate the intricate variables that I now know to be part of the equation. Indeed, there are "good" interpretations and "bad" ones. It's certainly not the interpretive Wild West, where rules are made up and anything goes. Rules of grammar matter, and the historical, cultural, and literary contexts affect the message of the text. But a reader's unique characteristics and experiences also affect things, albeit in relationship with the author's intentions. In addition, my formal education showed me that there are compositional realities pertaining to the canonization process of the biblical traditions that put texts in new historical and literary contexts. In turn, these new contexts come to affect a passage's message. In a word, I now realize that figuring out the message of the Bible may be more complicated that what we initially care to admit.

In my mind, therefore, one of the main questions for the student of the Bible transitions from, "Is everything legitimate?" to, "Are some interpretations 'better' than others?" In my opinion, the answer here is a resounding, "Yes!" Some interpretations are better, and better interpretations privilege a close reading of the text while giving appropriate attention to the literary, cultural, and historical dynamics associated with the passage. More specifically, better interpretations pay close attention to the grammatical and syntactical realities of the text. It's not just about individual words, but rather how words, in their grammatical forms, interact with other words at the clausal level. Better interpretations also give the necessary attention to a passage's immediate, book-level, canonical, historical, and cultural variables that inform the concepts, worldview, and conventions inherent to the text. Why do I believe these considerations result in "better" interpretations? Because I believe that God *used* ancient Israel to communicate his revelation of cosmic redemption.

Applied to Gen 1 and beyond, therefore, this results in a preference for interpretations that see these texts as an ancient Near

Eastern cosmological commentary. More specifically, I believe that interpretations that understand Gen 1–11 as polemical statements in response to the prevailing ideas of the Iron Age strike closest to the text's original intentions.[10] But specific to this project, any original intention could not have been about science or geology. Those lines of inquiry did not exist in the Iron Age. Rather, exposure to similar texts across the ancient world demonstrates that the intentions of these types of texts were to discuss the cosmos and the world's existential realities in terms of order (versus disorder) and other premodern or primitive concepts. To put it crudely, the authors of the biblical text were discussing things in terms that were widely familiar to the larger cultural milieu to establish a certain level of rapport on the way to subverting popular ideologies. Genesis 1–11 is not scientific. It's polemical.

And so, this brings me to my biggest concern with certain interpretive methods: the lack of cultural literacy. Because ancient Israel was an ancient Middle Eastern culture that demonstrated a remarkable amount of continuity with its neighbors (thank you, archaeology), possessing a certain capacity in understanding the prevailing culture, which ultimately includes their literary expressions, is nonnegotiable. Yet, there's more. When one realizes what was being said by Israel's neighbors—and how it was being said—one will also inevitably deal with questions of literary relationships. Whether it be Gen 1, Gen 3, the flood narrative, or something else, was there a literary relationship between what we read in the book of Genesis and in the larger textual corpus of the ancient world? Is one playing off the other? If so, why? Yes, it's a very complicated question to answer, but it's a question that one must consider when dealing with the texts of Gen 1–11. So, let's look at Gen 1–11 with a bit more detail.

10. Consequently, here I deviate from scholars like Davidson and Turner who don't distinguish a historical continuum between each legitimate textual layer. If certain historical-critical methodologies are used responsibly, it is possible to determine which layers encroached upon existing layers. For recent scholarly treatments in the content of Gen 1–11, see Arnold, "Holiness Redaction" 483–500. According to such a framework, a polemical function appears to be at the foundation of these texts.

4

Genesis 1–11: What's Going on Here?

GENESIS 1–11 IS A distinct unit of text that can be subdivided coherently. Those segments can be divided as follows: 1:1—2:3; 2:4—4:26; 5:1–32; 6:1—9:29; 10:1–32; 11:1–9; 11:10–32. Of these segments, 5:1–32, 10:1–32, and 11:10–32 are commonly referred to as genealogies, which, as we will see shortly, function very specifically. But initially, Gen 1:1—2:3 discusses the creation of the world in a very distinct manner. Marked by a quasi-poetic presentation, this segment details seven days wherein God Almighty coolly establishes order across various spheres of the cosmos. Most importantly, there is an observable parallelism to these days. In days 1–3, the spheres, or zones, of the world are created, and in days 4–6, the things that populate those spheres, or zones, are created. In the words of Arnold and Beyer,

> The narrative symmetry means that each day corresponds with a matching day. The creation of light (day 1) corresponds with the sun, the moon, and the stars to govern the use of light (day 4). The creation of sky (day 2) prepares the reader for day 5, in which God creates the birds. The narrative structure highlights days 3 and 6, in

Genesis 1–11: What's Going on Here?

which God makes the dry land and then creates animals and humankind to populate it.[1]

Day 1—Day and Night; Light	Day 4—Celestial Bodies
Day 2—Sky and Ocean	Day 5—Birds of the Air and Sea Creatures
Day 3—Separation of Land from Sea; Vegetation	Day 6—Land Animals with Humanity
Day 7—Rest	

On the seventh day, God rested as he blessed and consecrated his work, which is the terminus of this entire presentation. Again, Arnold writes:

> The recurrence of the creation formula and the symmetrical structure of the days of creation highlight the uniqueness of the day. As the climax of creation, God's sabbath rest is not what we normally think of as "rest," as though God needed a break from an exhausting job. Rather, the term fundamentally means "cessation," and implies also the celebration and completion of an accomplishment.[2]

The most important theme in this inaugural literary segment is instilling order and function. When Genesis begins, the reader is immediately told that a primordial disorder (*tōhū wabōhū*) existed alongside God's spirit.[3] However, with every utterance that follows in this chapter, God systematically instills order and overcomes the disorderly and unfunctional state. As stated by Sarna, "The quintessential point of the narrative is the idea of ordering that is the result of divine intent."[4] Eventually, the order that is created is emphatically described as "very good" (*tōv me 'ōd*). As for humanity in all of this, they are the culmination of God's creative actions,

---

1. Arnold and Beyer, *Encountering the Old Testament*, 54–55.
2. Arnold, *Encountering the Book of Genesis*, 24.
3. HALOT, 2:1689–90. See also Walton, *Genesis 1 as Ancient Cosmology*, 139–45; Walton, *Lost World of Genesis 1*, 46–53.
4. Sarna, *Genesis*, 6.

"images" (ṣelem) of the Creator (Gen 1:26–27). Yet, there was a responsibility imparted upon humanity: to exercise dominion over the created order.[5] In other words, the order of this creation is understood as a relationship between the Creator, humanity, and creation. Yet, between the Creator and humanity as the "image" of the Creator, the latter has the privilege of facilitating divine order upon creation. Or, as Moo and Moo have said, humanity is to "reflect his sovereignty throughout the earth."[6]

As for the issue of dominion, much has been said about this concept, and rightfully so. It's a complicated concept. Dominion as a responsibility of humanity stems from their job description offered in Gen 1:26–28. The NRSV reads:

> Then God said, "Let us make humankind in our image, according to our likeness; and let them have dominion over the fish of the sea, and over the birds of the air, and over the cattle, and over all the wild animals of the earth, and over every creeping thing that creeps upon the earth."
>
> So God created humankind in his image,
> in the image of God he created them;
> male and female he created them.
>
> God blessed them, and God said to them, "Be fruitful and multiply, and fill the earth and subdue it; and have dominion over the fish of the sea and over the birds of the air and over every living thing that moves upon the earth."

What makes the words "dominion" and "subdue" so difficult are the connotations that often accompany them. What the NRSV translates as "let them have dominion" is a verbal form from the

---

5. The syntax of the Hebrew communicates a result clause. I translate Gen 1:26 as, "And God said, 'Let us make humanity in our image, according to our likeness, so that they will rule the fish of the sea, the birds of the sky, the large animals, all the earth, and all the creeping animals which are creeping upon the earth.'"

6. Moo and Moo, *Creation Care*, 74

Genesis 1–11: What's Going on Here?

root *radāh* (רדה), which only appears twenty-three times in the Old Testament.[7] When it comes to Genesis, there are only two occurrences, and each of them are in this passage. While Nel distinguishes between positive and negative uses,[8] whereby the latter imports a connotation of domination or oppression, the only two "positive" occurrences are the Genesis occurrences here, which is a bit suspect on his part. Clearly, the occurrences in Gen 1 are different from the rest, but it's better to see this root as communicating the idea of facilitating a royal agenda versus creating sets of categories whereby one is filled solely by the occurrences in Genesis. Simply put, to "*radāh*" is better understood as "to rule in concert with a royal agenda." For example, when 1 Kgs 4:24 uses this verb to discuss the facilitation of Solomon's rule over the territories that he governed, it's not necessarily to communicate his harsh dominion or oppression. To put it another way, to say that a king "*radāhs*" over a territory does not mean, necessarily, that harshness, exploitation, or imperial ambitions are in play, although the occurrences of this root in Leviticus, Psalms, and Ezekiel recognize these possibilities. And with this in view, the appearance of this verb in Genesis appears akin to the general idea of facilitating a royal agenda. Thus, humanity, whose status as an "image" (*ṣelem*) of the Creator suggests that it functions as the conduit for a divinely royal agenda.

The issues with "subdue" are similar. However, the negative connotations that usually accompany *kabāš* (כבש) are even more intense. This root only appears fourteen times in the Old Testament,[9] and in Esth 7:8, it refers to a sexual assault. Elsewhere, slavery and imperial domination are referenced (2 Sam 8:11; Jer 34:11, 16; Neh 5:5; 2 Chr 28:10). Interestingly, the root is also used in Numbers, Joshua, and 1 Chronicles with respect to

---

7. Gen 1:26, 28; Lev 25:43, 46, 53; 26:17; Num 24:19; 1 Kgs 5:4, 30; 9:23; Isa 14:2, 6; 41:2; Ezek 29:25; 34:4; Joel 4:13; Pss 49:15; 68:28; 72:8; 110:2; Lam 1:13; Neh 9:28; 2 Chr 8:10.

8. Nel, "רָדָה," *NIDOTTE* 3:1056.

9. Gen 1:28; Num 32:22, 29; Josh 18:1; 2 Sam 8:11; Jer 34:11, 16; Mic 7:19; Zech 9:15; Esth 7:8; Neh 5:5; 1 Chr 22:18; 2 Chr 28:10.

subduing the land, which is something that Moo and Moo consider as a way to explain the Genesis usage (Num 32:22, 29; Josh 18:1; 1 Chr 22:18).[10] But in the end, Moo and Moo are correct to emphasize that the immediate context of this statement, let alone the Bible's overall witness to this matter, is critical to understanding the nature of this responsibility. Thus, these considerations "make impossible any interpretation of dominion in Gen 1:26-28 as domination, and it rules out any notion that God's entrusting of other creatures into our care mean that we may use them or the rest of creation however we like."[11] Thus, the relationship that appears to be envisioned is that of an orderly, perhaps an ambassadorial, relationship, which, incidentally, is significantly different that the picture that's created in the next textual segment.

The next literary segment within Gen 1–11 begins in 2:4, and it can be extended to 4:26. It again considers the elements of the creation event, but it also recounts humanity's fall as the apex of creation (Gen 3) as well as the aftermath of that devastating reconsideration (Gen 4). In total, Gen 2:4—4:26 progresses beyond a systematic account of an orderly creation to feature the emotional and relational aspects inherent to the created order. If God Almighty is presented in 1:1—2:3 as a straitlaced, matter-of-fact Creator who exists transcendently with humanity and the larger created order, in this segment of text he is more personal, intimate, and invested in his creation. Thus, the Lord God formed (*yaṣar*) humanity from the dust of the earth and blew into his nostrils the breath of life (Gen 2:7). Important are the verbs "form" and "breathe" in Gen 2:7: "Then the LORD God formed man from the dust of the ground, and breathed into his nostrils the breath of life; and the man became a living being" [my translation].

---

10. Moo and Moo, *Creation Care*, 76–77. They ponder if the allusion in Numbers and Joshua to "subduing the enemies of Israel" can allude to subduing the forces that prevent "bringing the earth under the appropriate rule of those who bear God's image." Moreover, they wonder to what extent this military metaphor could be appropriate to a post-Gen 3 world.

11. Moo and Moo, *Creation Care*, 79.

These verbs require proximity and intentionality, and the result of these two actions was the physical formation and motorization of humanity.

Yet, it's also important to realize that the intimacy between God and his creation goes beyond humanity. According to Gen 2:8–9, God plants a garden for humanity to live, and he causes vegetation and food to grow. This imagines a Creator with his sleeves rolled up to his elbows as he dirties his hands and forearms planting rows of food. It's substantially different that an authoritative voice uttering things into existence.

With respect to humanity's responsibilities, it continues the more personal and relational tone vis-à-vis Gen 1. The text reveals that humanity was tasked with caring for the garden (lit. "to work it and to preserve it"). Moreover, the animal kingdom appears to have been formed in pursuit of companionship. According to Gen 2:18–19, God formed (*yaṣar*) the animals because it was deemed that humanity should not be alone. Thus, the Creator sought for them a helper, and it was not until the realization set in that there was no suitable helper among the animals (v. 20) that God sent Adam into a deep sleep in order to create Eve. This bone of his bone, flesh of his flesh, would come to work alongside Adam as they fulfilled their responsibilities in the garden.

Yet in this chapter, boundaries are also discussed. In other words, as God explains Adam's responsibilities, he also details the limitations on his freedom. He is prohibited from partaking from one tree, the tree of the knowledge of good and evil (v. 17). In fact, this constitutes another important variation from Gen 1 that ultimately contributes to the differing tone. The choice to partake of the tree or to mind the prohibition imparts a sense of autonomy upon Adam and Eve that is different from the previous chapter.

Overall, the differences between Gen 1:1—2:3 and Gen 2:4–24 are substantial. Whether the characterization of the Creator or his creation, the order and content of creation, or the relationship between God and humanity, the history of biblical scholarship has shown an immense diversity in explaining these literary phenomena. Nevertheless, for the purposes of this project, I emphasize two things. First, Gen 2:4–24 constitutes a different perspective on the creation of the world. While it likely represents an earlier account than Gen 1:1—2:3,[12] Gen 2:4–24 focused upon humanity in the context of the created order, being intimate and personal. More importantly, and this is the second emphasis, the content of Gen 2:4–24 sets up chapters 3 and 4. The inevitable choice of whether humanity was going to honor the limits of their freedom falls front and center in chapter 3.

In chapter 3, the reader is introduced to an antagonist, the serpent. For reasons that are not quite clear, this creature approaches Eve to tempt her. The snake first questions (v. 1) the content of God's commands and then questions the stated outcome (vv. 4–5). From there, Eve's primal desires take over, and she eventually succumbs to the temptation. What's more, she entices Adam to partake in the disobedience (v. 6). The result? Not physical death, but a reversal of their blissful existence. They were still naked, but no longer unashamed. Rather, they became aware of their deficiencies and were embarrassed. Their eyes were opened, and their nakedness set in cognitively. Thus, they sewed plant leaves together as clothes (v. 7).

Of course, this turn of events does not elude the Creator. He eventually finds the two hiding and proceeds to interrogate Adam and Eve (vv. 8–13). After a few rounds of passing the buck, the truth is finally admitted. Thus, the punishment is levied. Indeed, much ink has been used in explaining various details about this chapter, whether in terms of the passage's theological or literary value. What's important here is that the order of creation is disrupted. Animosity between humanity and the animal kingdom is introduced (3:15), and the responsibilities and privileges that were allocated to humanity would instead because sources of anxiety and danger (vv. 16–19). Moreover, the space that was created for them was now forfeit. But perhaps most importantly, the residue of their disobedience would spill into the next generation. Consequently, when one reads about the jealousy, rivalry, and anger

---

12. For example, Arnold, " Genesis 1," 331–43.

between members of the first family in chapter 4, the reader is to understand this to be another effect of Gen 3.

Yet in spite of this hostility, humanity continues to multiply.

Chapter 5 is a genealogy, as are chapter 10 and a few other segments within Gen 1–11, for that matter (Gen 6:9; 11:10–26, 27–32). While we will discuss the importance of these shortly, suffice it to say for the moment that these texts function as bridges between major scenes. Thus, chapter 5 bridges the narrative gap between the first family and the flood narrative. Similarly, chapter 10 links the end of the flood narrative to the Tower of Babel episode. Speaking of the flood narrative, it constitutes the next major narrative segment within this literary unit. Countless articles and pages have been written on this, and it would be impossible to even survey the landscape in this project. Nevertheless, it's important to recognize for this project that the flood narrative carries forward the disorder of the fallen creation to a critical point. Apparently, things have devolved so badly that God expresses his remorse for his creation (6:6). Not only was humanity's wickedness pervasive, but perpetuating that wickedness was constantly at the forefront of humanity's mind (6:5). And it was this that spurred God to send a cataclysmic flood to wipe out humanity.

Now stop and think about that for a second. The world and humanity had gotten so bad that God wanted to do away with it.

Cutting against humanity's tendencies was one person: Noah. According to the biblical text, Noah's favor in the sight of the Lord (6:8) secured his salvation from the flood. Thus, the remainder of this narrative (6:9—9:17) recounts his family's efforts to honor the divine plan of salvation. They built a massive boat so that representatives of the entire animal kingdom could join them. They see the flood begin and end, and they safely exit the boat as it is stranded by the receding waters upon Mt. Ararat. All of this is commemorated with a sacrifice and an eternal covenant between Noah and God, wherein God vows never to revisit this cataclysmic event again. Yet, the symptoms of the broken creation persisted. This is clearly acknowledged in the account of Noah's drunkenness at the end of chapter 9 (vv. 18–29). Moreover, the sheer arrogance of humanity continued. In chapter 11, humanity gathers and endeavors to build a tower so tall that its top would reach heaven (Gen 11:1–4). And similar to the arrogant display of Gen 3, humanity is ultimately cast away from their space in order to wander throughout the land. As already alluded to, each of these scenes could be studied in isolation of each other. Each segment is clearly demarcated, and there's an internal coherence to each of them. However, in the context of Gen 1–11, the reader is to understand how all of them are working together for the sake of the entire unit. The quintessential proof of this is the strategic use of the so-called genealogies. Signaled by the use of the Hebrew term *tōledōt*, these literary features not only carry the narrative forward, but they also facilitate coherence between the segments.

To be more precise, the term *tōledōt* appears seven times throughout Gen 1–11 (2:4; 5:1; 6:9; 10:1; 10:32; 11:10; 11:27), and it comes from the root *yodh-lamed-dalet*, which often conveys the idea of "birth." Thus, *tōledōt* could be translated as "begettings" or "generations."[13] Indeed, this term often introduces genealogical listings, but as Gen 2:4 shows, this is not always the case. Nevertheless, the *tōledōt* certainly ensure that the transitions between scenes in Gen 1–11 remain efficient. And in many instances, particularly when a genealogical listing follows, focus remains, in the subsequent narration, on important people upon whose backs God's plan of redemption continues. As stated by Sarna, "[The *tōledōt* introduce] what follows, invariably in close connection with the name of a person already mentioned in the narrative. [Their] use indicates that a new and significant development is at hand."[14]

Without a doubt, these lists are not functioning as strict chronological markers, as if numerical values applied to each name on the list are added together to calculate the age of the earth or something like that. There are two main reasons for this.[15] First, genealogical lists didn't function in this way in antiquity. Arnold emphasizes a more natural social function, particularly in

---

13. Sarna, *Genesis*, 16
14. Sarna, *Genesis*, 16
15. Arnold, "Genesis Narratives," 32–33.

oral societies. Specific to Genesis, therefore, they are largely fluid mechanisms that provide social identification for the people that will function strategically in the context of God's redemptive purposes. They certainly contain some historiographic material, but that is not their primary function. Second, the use of genealogies was common across the ancient Near East, and they never functioned primarily as a historiographic source. Indeed, Arnold is correct to note subtle deviations between the biblical usage and the standard usage through the ancient Near East—that is, the biblical usage does not appear to have the overt political and apologetic function as is often the case across antiquity—but the functional differences do not equate to a historiographic function as the primary function.

All of this begins to imply something about the presence of ages in the biblical lists. If the lists are not to be used as precise data points for historical reconstruction, then what is the function of noting the ages of people in those lists? A telling comparison appears in the Sumerian King List.[16] This Sumerian catalog from the second or third millennium BCE that robotically lists kings and their cities begins with a notation that the institution of kingship came down from heaven. Right there, the apologetic purpose of this Mesopotamian list becomes crystal clear, but it also proceeds to list names of kings and the length of their reigns. And boy, are those reigns long. Individual reigns include 28,800 years, 36,000 years, 64,800 years, 43,200 years, and 21,000 years. However, in line 39, there is a notation of "the flood" consuming the land. Interestingly, after that notation in the Sumerian account, the length of individual reigns steadily declines to the point that, by the end of the list, the lengths of royal reigns are rather reasonable. A similar phenomenon can be observed in the biblical text. Prior to the flood narrative, the names in these *tōledōt* live several hundred years. After the flood narrative, lives that had lasted past 900 years steadily give way to lives of only about a hundred or so. While lives of 100-plus are still difficult to process given what is known about the average life expectancy in antiquity, these final figures are a

16. Jacobsen, *Sumerian King List*. See also *Sumerian Kings List*.

lot more manageable. Could it be that at least part of the function of these *tōledōt* was to highlight general anthropological development before and after a memorable diluvian event? Or perhaps the collaboration of a flood narrative with a genealogical listing was an accepted literary mechanism used to contextualize a culture's current context with a glorified ancient past?

Speaking of memorable diluvian events, the biblical flood account is perhaps the most famous event in the Bible's story. Growing up in church, Noah, the flood, and all the animals getting on the ark was a Bible story that you discussed as soon as kids left the nursery. Scholastically, there may be more commentary on the flood narrative than any other passage in all of Scripture. And this is not just because this account is theologically significant. As Carol Hill and company have demonstrated, the flood narrative intersects with geological conversations and questions about the age of the earth.[17] But without a doubt, the single most influential catalyst for establishing the flood narrative as one of the most popular narratives in the Bible was the discovery of the Mesopotamian flood narrative. While this is not the context to recount the story of how it was discovered among a hoard of cuneiform tablets in the British Museum,[18] one must understand the overwhelming amount of continuity between the biblical and Mesopotamian flood narratives. Most obviously, each account highlights a divinely sanctioned deluge which almost wipes out humanity. Of the humans that survived, there is a protagonist who constructs a boat to be the vehicle of salvation. Moreover, each account links the flood to the decision of the diety(ies), and after the flood subsides and the boat comes to rest on a high mountain, sacrifices are given by the remaining humans and there is a "sign" offered in truce. In other words, the biblical and Mesopotamian flood accounts share a narrative outline.

---

17. Hill et al., *Grand Canyon*.
18. See Schreiner, *Pondering the Spade*, 35–53.

Genesis 1–11: What's Going on Here?

Tablet 11 of the Gilgamesh Epic, Also Known as the Flood Tablet; British Museum

Yet, never fear! There are also very significant differences. The Mesopotamian account assumes a polytheistic worldview in contrast to the Bible's monotheistic one, which of course has important implications for the tone of each account. Thus, there is backbiting and rivalry among the gods in the Mesopotamian account, and at one point, the Mesopotamian deities act like scared dogs in the middle of a thunderstorm. For the Bible, God is always cool, in control, and rational. Perhaps most interestingly, one knows exactly why the flood occurs in the Bible. It's not clear why the gods decide to send the flood in the Mesopotamian account. Less significantly, but important to the overall presentation, the protagonist in the Mesopotamian account is sneaky and actually brings on board his boat craftsmen and cultural artifacts alongside the animals. This suggests a concern for the continuity of the popular culture, which is something that God wants to squash in the biblical account.

I could go on and on listing the similarities and the differences, and many people have. The result is a massive catalog of convergences and divergences that demand an explanation. Quite simply, what gave rise to such a stunning connection? On the one hand, many people explain this historically, as if both accounts actually testify to a singular historical event. If so, then there's a follow-up question: "Which one was first?," or, "Which one derived from the other?" When I ask my students about such a scenario, there is a bit of diversity among the answers. However, almost universally, there is also a statement confirming that whatever happened, the Bible's account is the one that is "true." If anything, the Mesopotamian account is the "wrong" account of the event.

However, there's something more nuanced here. It's important to note that the similarities largely align with the narrative outline. The differences align with the details of the narratives, to the point where some of my more perceptive students essentially ask, "Are we really talking about the same narrative?" Considering the nature of the similarities and the differences, therefore, one realizes that there's a sophisticated interaction between these two textual traditions. It's more than just one coming first or one getting it "right" where the other gets it "wrong." Instead, I believe the biblical account was likely written after the Mesopotamian text and in full awareness of it.[19] The biblical writers, therefore, fashioned their story with just enough similarity to ensure that the

---

19. There are two reasons for this historical relationship. First, the textual tradition of the Mesopotamian account reaches centuries before Israel became a polity. Second, the textual tradition of the Mesopotamian account demonstrates translation into multiple languages and wide dissemination, particularly during the Iron Age. For the classic treatment of these variables, see Tigay, *Evolution of the Gilgamesh Epic*.

popular account would be recalled by the audience, akin to how late Christian Gen-Xers and early Christian millennials hear Dan Smith's "Baby Got Book" and immediately recall Sir Mix A Lot's "Baby Got Back." When this happened, the theology of the biblical writer, emphasized through the differences, would attack and ultimately undermine the theology of the other account.

The final segment of this unit is the Tower of Babel episode. It's a narrative about the collaboration of humanity on the plain of Shinar. Their desire was to show their collective might by building a city that featured an installation akin to a modern-day skyscraper as a monument to themselves. However, these plans struck a chord. According to the text, God believed any success would translate into unbridled ambition and hubris. Therefore, to prevent this, he struck humanity with language confusion. The result? They had no choice but to abandon the project. On the one hand, the reader could look at this and say, "Ah! This is how different languages came to be!" However, when one understands referents assumed by this narrative, such as ziggurats and the social and economic impact of urban centers, the reader will likely realize that this scene brings to a culmination the degradation of humanity's relationship to the larger created order and its unique relationship with the Creator.

There is widespread consensus that the "tower" of Gen 11 is a ziggurat. These pyramid-like structures offered no hollow core, but were filled with dirt. They ranged in size but always featured a stairway or ramp reaching to the top of the edifice where there was often a small room that functioned as a domicile for the deity. However, scholars attest that while that space did function as sacred space, it was not a locus of any ritualistic action. Thus, the belief was that the deity would "come down" (vs. the people "going up"). This is what Gen 11:5–7 says happened. In fact, the text reveals that when God came down to assess their efforts, he was offended to the point of action. God didn't like what he saw.

So, what did he see? Well, the text is not quite clear. But based on the linkage of building a tower with "making a name" for themselves (v. 4), perhaps the disappointment was linked to what the construction signified: arrogance. Perhaps there is also an undertone of coercion, as if the presence of the tower would coerce the deity to come down. Whatever exactly was the issue, the explicit link between construction and fame is a telling development to humanity's relationship with their Creator. They no longer understand their function to be representatives, or "images" of the Creator. Rather their work bears witness to themselves, to their capabilities as a species.

In sum, the message of Gen 1–11 is the result of connecting several smaller narratives, each with their own integrity, by means of diverse transitional passages and genealogies. The result is a picture of the world that features a dramatic fall from grace that only metathesizes as the unit progresses. However, in spite of the degenerating situation, God did not restart his creation from scratch. Rather, he chose to preserve his crowning achievement in order to work with and in spite of them, in the context of this fallen world, to eventually redeem it all. Thus, the acts of grace and mercy, the salvation of people, and the covenant with a small remnant to repopulate the world can't be suffocated by the prevailing devolution of humanity. Yet, there's more to consider. Many of these scenes and literary features echo across the ancient Near Eastern literary corpus. While some are clearer than others, motifs, themes, and even narratives are similar to what is found in other textual catalogs of cultures across the Fertile Crescent. What can be seen, therefore, is a literary modus operandi that exploits popular concepts and frames of reference in order to subvert them. Close study of these similar texts not only demonstrate similarities and differences but also convergences and divergences that target prevailing ideas of the larger culture.

If this interpretive discussion is on target, then it's clear that Gen 1 and beyond are incredibly intentional in their discussions. They present a culturally conditioned commentary on the present state of humanity and the world. Again, according to these texts, the world currently exists in a state of disorder because of humanity's arrogance. Indeed, there's a Creator who values his creation so much that he ultimately decided not to start over but see it restored. Nevertheless, the text is also clear that in this very long and complicated journey, the Creator will face obstacles along the way. In fact, the reader may think from time to time that the Creator's efforts are counterproductive. The disorder is so deeply ingrained in creation and humanity that his redemptive efforts are repeatedly undermined by his creation. Thus, the commentary offered in Gen 1–11 is overtly theological, even polemical, as it not only provides an alternative to prevailing ideas about the world and its state, but it also tries to persuade its audience. It's not scientific or biological.[20]

To be completely transparent, an awareness of various ancient Near Eastern texts was an important catalyst for me to shift from what can only be described as a more fundamentalistic understanding of Gen 1 and beyond to where I am now. When I realized that other narratives existed from the ancient world and that they said similar things about the same topics, merely stating that one derived from another or even perverted the other (or that the "true" account came from Moses) ultimately struck me as both simplistic and naive. And let me be clear: this was not because I lost my faith or adopted a lower view of Scripture. Rather, it's because I came to appreciate more the complicated realities of literary development and literary relationships in the ancient world as well as ancient Israel's place within a larger cultural river.

Another catalyst for the development of my position was learning Hebrew. Consider vv. 11–12 and v. 24 of Gen 1. In these texts, the Hebrew reads as follows.

> Gen 1:11–12: God said, "May the earth sprout [*tadšē'*] vegetation—that is, plants bearing seeds, and fruit trees bearing fruit (wherein its seed is)—upon the earth with respect to their kind." And it was so. The earth produced [*tōṣē'*] vegetation, plants bearing seeds with respect to their kind as well as trees bearing fruit (wherein its seed is) with respect to its kind. And God saw that it was good [my translation].

---

20. On the difference between polemical theology and texts functioning as "counter texts," see Walton, "Interactions," 334.

Gen 1:24: God said, "May the earth produce [*tōṣē'*] living creatures with respect to their kind, working animals, creeping animals, and earthly creatures with respect to their kind." And it was so [my translation].

In these verses, there are two significant verbs: *tadšē'* (v. 11) and *tōṣē'* (vv. 12 and 24). In each occurrence, the definite noun "the earth" is the subject of the verb, and a catalog of vegetation and animals exist as the objects. Written in the Hiphil stem, therefore, these verbs imply causation. Thus, these verses can essentially be translated, "God says, 'May the earth cause vegetation to sprout,' and 'May the earth bring forward creatures.'"

I will never forget the moment when I realized the potential of these statements. I was sitting in my OT 605: Old Testament Theology class at Asbury Theological Seminary. The professor was lecturing and progressing through a grammatical explanation of the opening chapters of Genesis. When he emphasized the causative nature of these verbs, I anxiously raised my hand.

"If it's a Hiphil, then there is an emphasis upon God *causing* the earth to produce these creatures and foliage, right?"

"Yes."

"So what does this mean for evolution? Does it mean that the biblical text allows for conversations about evolutionary theory?"

As I remember, he never definitively answered my question. However, in my mind, his evasion was moot to these remarkable grammatical realities. To put it bluntly, the semantic framework of the biblical text allows for the attribution of agency upon the created order. By implication, in my mind, the concept of evolution is something that need not be antagonistic to the Christian faith.

Now, indeed, there is a line here. In fact, this highlights one of the severe deficiencies of Darwin's ideas of natural selection vis-à-vis Christian theology. Just as there is agency imparted upon the earth, this chapter also makes it very clear that God's agency is the genesis of it all. In other words, while the mechanisms of the creative agency are more diverse than many fundamentalists care to admit, the text hangs on to divine agency as foundational to the mysterious process.

So, what does this all mean for Ken Ham and other vehement proponents of Young Earth creationism, or any other militant proponent of their respective interpretive theory?

Simple. Tread lightly.

The messages of Gen 1 and beyond is incredibly sophisticated, but also culturally conditioned. They are products of a distinct culture living in a particular part of the world at a particular moment. They are also products of a culture that perceived the world in a certain way, and they used those perceptions to engage their larger culture. Thus, one's interpretive conclusions, whatever they may be, *must* honor these realities in some way. So, if you are using these texts to make statements about the origins of the world and humanity, you can't usurp the original intentions of the text. If you do, you are proceeding down a road that may ask the Bible to bear a weight that it was not designed to bear. Or, if I may be so bold, if you are using these texts to make statements about the origins of humanity and the world, you must acknowledge that those biblical statements are limited by cultural perceptions and worldviews.

5

Seal Lions Bites and Frigatebirds

ON BOTH OCCASIONS WHEN we went to the Galápagos Islands, my brother-in-law had arrived there several weeks ahead of us as he was leading a group of students on a university trip. Asbury University's Biogeography of the Galápagos Islands spends a few weeks traveling between islands as they discuss issues of evolution, biology, ecology, and the history of the islands. One night shortly before our departure, Ginny was talking to Ben on the phone. Here is half the phone conversation that I observed:

"How is it over there?"

Inaudible response

"I really *want* to see sea lions! Will we see sea lions?"

Inaudible response-

"*Really*? Oh no! But I really want to see them!"

Inaudible response

"You're mean."

After Ginny hung up the phone, I asked her about the conversation.

"Why did you get frustrated with Ben? What did he say?"

She proceeded to tell me that he was being incredibly sarcastic. Now, sarcasm happens to be a spiritual gift that runs in the

Brammell family. It, however, has a particularly potent manifestation in my brother-in-law. He was apparently channeling this gift when he told her that he was unsure if we would see sea lions as they were quite rare throughout the archipelago.

His comments couldn't be farther from the truth. San Cristóbal Island, which is one of the more famous islands in the chain, boasts one of the world's large congregations of Galápagos sea lions. In other words, Ben was telling his sister, in a very Brammell way, that it would be impossible to not see sea lions. More precisely, he should have said we would be hard-pressed not to *step* on sea lions as we walked through Puerto Baquerizo Moreno. Sea lions are everywhere.

During our 2023 trip, we spent a majority of our trip on San Cristóbal Island. As one of the most popular islands in the archipelago, it's home to Aeropuerto de San Cristóbal that ferries passengers on and off the islands. One of the easternmost islands, it was formed like all the rest of the islands, through the fusion of several volcanic hot spots as tectonic plates migrated. This island, with its main city of Puerto Baquerizo Moreno, is also the capital of the province. Puerto Baquerizo Moreno was settled in the mid-nineteenth century, and today it thrives on fishing and tourism. In fact, it's a town that one would imagine if they are trying to envision a Latin American coastal town. A breeze constantly blows off the water, and the narrow streets, which are dotted with local business ventures, all seem to have their terminus at the waterfront. There are numerous bays, where people can lounge around and watch the ocean life and boats. The hub of the town revolves around the main bay that controls maritime business and general water traffic. But without a doubt, one of the city's claims to fame is that the large population of *Zalophus wollebaeki* practically run the town.

Zalophus wollebaeki, the scientific name for the Galápagos sea lion, lives almost exclusively on the Galápagos Islands. They can grow up to approximately eight feet in length and weigh up to around 850 pounds, depending on the sex of the animal. Males are much bigger than females, and males also display a prominent bump on their foreheads. Yet, both sexes are known for their distinct physiology that allows them to "gallop" over land, which is made possible by swinging their hind flipper under their pelvic girdle as they move across land. This iconic motion produces the awkward (but very effective) galloping motion. And when it comes to their presence on the island, they are ubiquitous. They lay on boat docks, lounge around in drainage canals, and even sleep on city benches. They are omnipresent. They flop around and offer a rather formidable roar if you get too close. Yet at night, that's when they are most impressive. In Puerto Baquerizo Moreno, they are known to congregate on the city's beaches and join in unison to offer one of the most awful, ear-piercing orgies of sound that you will ever hear. I honestly don't know how anyone who stays at a hotel along the harbor road gets any sleep, even with the doors and windows closed. It's *so loud*.

When you initially see them, sea lions look relatively harmless. Truthfully, they strike you as incredibly slothful. They just lay there, minding their own business. Often, they appear to be sleeping. But they can go zero to sixty on the agitation scale in about half a second.

One evening, the family was enjoying a walk along the harborfront in Puerto Baquerizo Moreno. We eventually made our way onto one of the boat piers as we wanted to go to its end, stare into the water, and listen to the sounds of the bay. However, we apparently got too close to a sea lion that was silently sleeping on a bench in the middle of the pier. It was dark and we couldn't really see anything, but apparently someone said something too loud. In an instant, what I swore was only a log reared its head, bared its teeth, and let out one of the loudest barks I have ever heard. If the sea lion could speak English, it would have undoubtedly said something like, "Get the hell away from me! I'll kill you!" We all almost soiled ourselves. But more importantly, once the shock of being violently threatened wore off, we remembered something very important, a lesson that was drilled into my wife and my brother-in-law by their veterinarian father but had slipped our minds because of the excitement of just being on the Galápagos Islands: these are wild animals, and they share space with humans. As such, there's a delicate balance which can go sideways very quickly. Nevertheless, this was not the most unsettling experience that involved sea lions during our trip. That happened at Playa Mann.

Playa Mann is a relatively small beach that sits just off Avenida Alsacio Northia, right across the street from Universidad San Fransisco de Quito and the Galápagos Science Center. It's a peaceful location that looks westward into the sunset and features the rhythms of crashing waves. Yet it's a beach that is shared with sea lions. Whether they are swimming among the humans in the shallow bay water or just lounging in the sand on the northern portion of the beach, the interaction between the mammalian species is usually peaceful, even playful. However, on one occasion, a couple of male sea lions engaged in a show of masculinity.

This began on the northern parts of the beach to our right as we looked out over the bay. When they started their show, they were nowhere close to anybody. But slowly and surely the conflict intensified and eventually made its way southward toward the human beachgoers. Truth be told, the people who were aware of what was transpiring saw things coming. The barks and snaps became more and more violent. Finally, the two six-hundred-pound (or more) males began chasing each other and wrestling as they went. In no more than a few short moments, the human mothers began rushing over to their small children to scoop them up and run out of the way. Eventually, the show of masculinity had developed into a full-fledged brawl that spilled into other parts of Playa Mann. Spanish, English, or French, it didn't matter. Everyone was yelling, and everyone knew what was being said. "Watch out! Sea lions! They's fighting... and they're coming right toward you! You are going to get run over!"

If it wasn't so scary, it would have been funny. Snarling, saliva, and yelps of pain help paint the picture of this experience. There was real hostility between these two males, and everyone was trying not to get caught up in the mix—everyone except one couple whose sunbathing apparently would not be deterred by any pugnacious sea lions. The potential of being squashed by two six-hundred-pound sea lions was not enough of a deterrent, and the males missed them only by inches. Ben and I watched all this transpire. It was somewhat surreal, actually, and we breathed a sigh of relief when that couple *finally* decided to move. Oddly, it was only after the two somersaulting sea lions moved past them.

Galápagos Sea Lions Lying on Playa Mann.

San Cristóbal Island is also home to the Monumento a Charles Darwin. This monument sits atop a hill named Cerro Tijeretas, or "Frigatebird Hill," that overlooks a small bay, which happens to offer one of the most intimate snorkeling adventures among the Galápagos Islands. It's called Bahia Baquerizo Moreno, "the Bay of Baquerizo Moreno." There, you swing with tropical fish, sea turtles, and sea lions. In fact, the ocean animals will swim within arm's length of you. And in the case of the sea lions, they approach you only to stare quizzically while they float upside down. It's as if they are saying, "What's your deal?" It's really amazing, and it couldn't be less intimidating. That is, unless you get too close to the sea lions while they are sleeping, which is exactly what happened to our middle child.

We were coming out of the bay after some snorkeling only to find the walkway out of the water blocked by three female lions taking a nap. When Bailey saw them, she stopped. Then she looked at me. She didn't have to say anything. Her eyes said it. "Dad? What do I do? They're in the way." I told her not to worry about it, but just don't step on them. I assured her that if she didn't bother them, they wouldn't bother her. I went on to tell her to be assertive and just walk over them. That's what I did, and I was hoping that she would follow suit. Well, she followed suit, all right. But as she was stepping over one of those sea lions, it turned its head, opened its mouth, and quickly bit Bailey's lower leg. I saw it happening, but I could only just stare as that mouth enclosed her leg and those teeth bore down. Of our three kids, it would be Bailey that would get bitten. Not Maddie. Not Lily. Bailey.

Now, before you judge me, I will attempt to justify my negligence by saying that it turned out to be only a playful nip. It left a red mark where the teeth were, but only slightly. Most importantly, the skin wasn't broken and there was no blood. However, the cries and tears, even a bit of wailing, suggested that staples, stitches, perhaps even a metal plate to fuse bone back together, were in order.

When you go to the Galápagos Islands, there's an intimacy with the animal kingdom that is second to none. In fact, it's one of the main reasons why people even go there. Indeed, you experience several species that are endemic to that region. You get to see things that only live there! But it's the proximity of the interaction that really puts the experience over the top. There are no pens, cages, or barriers. If you want to get bitten by a sea lion even, it could very well happen! If you want to touch a Galápagos tortoise, you just have to catch up to one and touch it (they are actually faster than you would initially guess . . . but you're really not supposed to touch them). But if these interactions with the sea lions reinforced anything, it's the delicacy of the relationship. As we experienced, there's a fine line between playful interaction and barks that function as a warning to "Get back!" Indeed, this is not unique to the Galápagos Islands, but our trip in the summer of 2023 drove this point home in a way that I had never experienced.

And I'm not the only person that marvels over this. Many biologists note the unique interactions on the Galápagos Islands. And when it comes to the interactions between humanity and sea lions, it's been the focus of several important studies. In fact, a relatively recent article published by Denkinger and a group of researchers, the "Urban Life of Galápagos Sea Lions," effectively speaks to these variables.[1] In this article, the authors note that 13 percent of all Galápagos sea lions live on San Cristóbal Island, and a large majority of those live in the vicinity of Wreck Bay, which is the bay at the heart of Puerto Baquerizo Moreno. Consequently, the researchers highlight that the Galápagos sea lions essentially "share their resting beaches with tourism and other activities," which is a reality that drives this intimate contact with approximately 30,000 residents and 185,000 visitors across all the islands.[2] On the one hand, this certainly creates a surreal experience of literally stepping over a sea lion or being serenaded by their barks as you make your way along the oceanfront at night. On the other hand, this intimate proximity translates to new threats and hostilities. Denkinger and company have noted an increase in human-caused injury and mortality rates among Galápagos sea lions: "Human interaction is leading to negative consequences for the Galápagos sea lion population of Wreck Bay. . . . The observed growing number of human-related mortality and injuries highlights a potential risk for the long-term viability of this colony."[3] And this dynamic "produces changes in their behavior."[4] Yet, direct impact between humans and Galápagos sea lions is not the only trend associated with the blurring of habitats. Ruiz-Saenz and his team have noted the rising number of canine distemper infections among Galápagos sea lions.[5] Such infections can be fatal and are linked to the rise in the number of domesticated dogs on the islands.

Consequently, there's an irony at the heart of the allure of the Galápagos Islands. While it's one of the most appealing and pristine environments in the world, with every visitor or increase

1. Denkinger et. al., "Urban Life," 10–14.
2. Denkinger et. al., "Urban Life," 10.
3. Denkinger et. al., "Urban Life," 12
4. Denkinger et. al., "Urban Life," 13
5. Ruiz-Saenz et. al., "Seroconversion," 1–9.

in human contact, a fundamental alteration to that environment happens. What once was is lost. Indeed, the change that happens could be beneficial, but that pristine environment has irrevocably changed.

A Galápagos Sea Lion Relaxing in the Sun.

As I have reflected upon this dynamic, my mind eventually settles upon a few passages in Genesis. This first is arguably one of the most famous passages in all the Bible: Gen 3:15. Speaking to the serpent, God Almighty states, "Hostility I will put between you and the women, between your offspring and her offspring; they will strike your head, and you will strike their head" [my translation]. Among those who are familiar with this passage, most recognize it for its prophetic association with Christ. In fact, it's often referred to as the *protoevangelium*, or the "first good news." In this vein, when I read this passage, there's a part of me that thinks of the opening scene in Mel Gibson's *The Passion of the Christ*, where a distraught Jesus stomps on the head of a slithering serpent as he accepts his responsibility to go to the cross on behalf of humanity.

Yet, in its plain sense, this passage addresses the consequences of the deception and defiance that had just transpired. Genesis 3:14–19 is a series of curses, and some of them speak to a developing hostility between humanity and the animal kingdom in the aftermath of things. Not only is the first word in the Hebrew ordering of Gen 3:15 "hostility," but this verse climaxes in a volley of curses pronounced against the serpent for its part in humanity's original rebellion (Gen 3:14–15). Moreover, there is a significant discussion about how to translate these clauses, which inevitably highlights the prominence of interspecies hostility as a reality of existence moving forward. Consider the New International Version's translation of this verse: "And I will put enmity between you and the woman, and between your offspring and hers; he will crush your head, and you will strike his heel." Important are the verbs "crush" and "strike." According to the NIV translation, while the serpent will only strike humanity, humanity will crush the serpent. This may suggest a more violent reaction by humanity. More importantly, however, the juxtaposition of "crush" and "strike" suggests that two different Hebrew verbs are behind the English translation. In reality, the same Hebrew verb is behind both English verbs. To its credit, the NIV offers an alternative translation of "strike" for "crush" in the footnote, but burying this reality in a footnote does little to clarify the semantics. The reality is that most people don't look at these notes. Rather, as Hamilton states, "In order to maintain the duplication of the Hebrew verb, whatever English equivalent one decides on must be used twice."[6] The result? A mutually violent hostility between particular species characterizes their existence moving forward.

Despite the complicated linguistic discussions about how to translate verbs, it seems clear that the biblical writer is recognizing an animosity between humanity and its reptilian counterpart. Moreover, he is linking it to the repercussions of humanity's waywardness. To put it another way, the Bible is arguing that the created order collaborated with humanity to produce the current state of existence, and said state can be described as one built upon

---

6. Hamilton, *Book of Genesis*, 1:197. Hamilton offers a very important examination of the grammatical and semantic difficulties of this verse. See 1:197–200.

hostility and reciprocal violence. But there's more. The biblical writer will later describe the "dread of humanity" falling upon the animal kingdom *in toto* (see below). Therefore, the Bible is recognizing not just a reciprocal hostility but also a systemic hostility. It's a hostility that is localized in the interaction between certain species, but it will also impact the entire created order. It is in light of this that Drew Johnson is correct: "The biblical authors conceived of the cosmos as currently unnatural or, as some say, denatured."[7] Simply put, this state of hostility is not what was intended.

It's my conviction that the studies just mentioned regarding the human impact on the Galápagos sea lion population (see above), as well as my family's vacation anecdotes, bear witness to this reciprocal and sometimes hostile interaction among species. These studies and experiences show that humanity's concern for advancing its presence and way of life on the island chain, which includes both leisure and economic development, results in close and significant contact that produces a range of effects. The nipping of Bailey's leg—as if to merely say, "You're getting too close"—is symptomatic of contact that is crossing boundaries and, more than anything, increased annoyance. However, the presence of canine distemper virus in the sea lion population testifies to something more adversarial, perhaps even an existential threat linked to the presence of humanity and its way of life. Yet, the hostility within the created order is not limited to humanity and reptiles, nor humanity and everything else. Again, the Galápagos Islands offer a unique context to see a different kind of hostility in action.

There are two types of frigatebirds in the Galápagos Islands: the magnificent frigatebird (*Fregata magnificens*) and the great frigatebird (*Fregata minor*). Both species are difficult to distinguish, and both make a habit of nesting near bodies of water in tall trees or rock ledges. Impressively, they are known to travel hundreds, if not thousands, of miles away from their breeding grounds. Physiologically, certain features, such as their hollow bones, make them

---

7. Johnson, *What Hath Darwin*, 43. For his conversation on the term's nature and its derivatives according to the conceptual worlds of the Bible and the natural sciences, see 42–48.

very light, thereby creating the ability to sore and fly for days. They are incredibly efficient and require only a minimal amount of food. Their wingspans can exceed six feet, but the most iconic physical feature is the bright red chest that puffs out during mating rituals.

Nevertheless, what distinguishes them the most in the animal kingdom is the relationship they have with other avian marine life. Nelson has called them "opportunistically predatory."[8] They take eggs, even young birds, from other species. They have also been known to consume turtle hatchlings. Most interestingly, they are more precisely described as kleptoparasitic. That is, they steal food honestly caught by other avian species, an act of piracy that can be accomplished by attacking their victims in midair, on the ground, or, in some cases, in the water.

I remember the first time I saw a frigatebird. I was looking up and I noticed a bird with V-shaped tail and unusually long wingspan effortlessly soaring in the air, presumably riding the air currents. The grace and efficiency of its movement was impressive.

Frigatebird Flying.

---

8. Nelson, *Pelicans, Cormorants, and their Relatives*, 553.

"Hey Ben! What is that bird up there?"
"I'm pretty sure it's a frigatebird."
"Look at the size of those wings!"

Later in the trip, I observed one nesting at the top of a tree, overlooking a small bay at Cerro Brujo. Again, it was impressive. While it was not blowing out its bright red chest, you could see a bright red spot on its chest. The color just jumped out. But I was taken aback at the annoyance of our excursion guide when I asked him what species of bird I was admiring sitting atop of the tree.

"What kind of bird is that?" I asked.
"Up there?"
"Yeah. I mean, look at it! That's a great picture."
"Oh. That's just a frigatebird."

You really could hear his disappointment. It was as if he was thinking, "Stupid American tourist. He's getting all excited about one of the biggest pests on the island." I am almost positive that he was thinking this because he spent the next ten minutes describing how the frigatebirds attack other birds, like the various booby species, in order to steal their food. Apparently, the attacks of the frigates produce so much stress and anxiety that the victims will vomit up their recently eaten food, at which point the frigates feast on the vomit.

Seal Lions Bites and Frigatebirds

Frigatebird Overlooking Cerro Brujo.

Conversations about hostility between species have always been at the heart of biological discourse, and it usually happens under the guise of "competition." Perhaps, even more colloquially, it's the "survival of the fittest." Regardless of the specific term or phrase used, it refers to an antagonism and aggression between species over resources and habitats. In fact, competition has been discussed alongside mutation as one of the fundamental tenets of biological discourse. Darwin himself highlighted the central role of competition in his *Origin of Species*:

> All organic beings are exposed to severe competition.... Nothing is easier than to admit in words the truth of the universal struggle for life, or more difficult—at

least I found it so—than constantly to bear this conclusion in mind. Yet unless it be thoroughly ingrained in the mind, the whole economy of nature, with every fact on distribution, rarity, abundance, extinction, and variation, will be dimly seen or quite misunderstood. We behold the face of nature bright with gladness, we often see superabundance of food; we do not see or we forget that the birds which are idly singing round us mostly live on insects or seeds, and are thus constantly destroying life; or we forget how largely these songsters, or their eggs, or their nestlings, are destroyed by birds and beasts of prey; we do not always bear in mind, that, though food may be now superabundant, it is not so at all seasons of each recurring year.[9]

However, biological discourse subsequent to Darwin has repeatedly nuanced the prominence of competition by considering the degree to which cooperation also stimulates development. Famously, Ashely Montagu described the prominence of Darwin's natural selection as the determining variable for biological development as "Darwin's Fallacy."[10] More recently, Martin Nowak went as far as to articulate a set of rules that determine how cooperation functions alongside competition to stimulate biological development.[11]

Consequently, among those who specialize in understanding how species interact and affect each other, the issue of competition and hostility is not only an ongoing one, but it's also one that's being revised, albeit at varying degrees. What is not being revised is how the Bible testifies to a hostility being woven into the fabric of creation. I have already discussed Gen 3:15 above, but Gen 9:2 also speaks to this. Having just blessed Noah and his family in the wake of the flood, and having exhorted them to "be fruitful, increase, and fill the earth" (9:1), the Lord also declares that

9. Darwin, *On the Origin of Species*, 50–51.
10. Montagu, *Darwin*.
11. Nowah, "Five Rules," 1560–63. Even here, it must be stated that cooperation is never truly altruistic.

humanity's fearful terror[12] would "be upon all the living creatures of the earth." This is significant. The flood, which functioned as a type of creational "reset," was not so absolute as to nullify the full effects of sin in general, nor the hostility between species specifically, that had evolved in the wake of humanity's hubris and sin. Moreover, as mentioned above, this verse can be understood to bear witness to the increasing hostility between elements within the created order. In other words, the hostility between humanity and one particular element of the animal kingdom has spread and intensified to include "the birds of the sky, everything that creeps on the ground, and all the fish of the sea" (Gen 9:2).

Yet, as this fearful terror was pronounced to be a perpetual reality of the created order, according to the Bible, it also exists in the crosshairs of God's redemptive plan.[13] In other words, the intentions of God's plan of redemption involve absolving this ingrained hostility. As already mentioned, this speaks to the Christian perception that the created order currently exists in an "unnatural state." It is unnatural because it's currently functioning in a perverted or fundamentally defective way. It deviates from the way it is supposed to be.

And in the end, one is forced to consider if this is another tension between Christian discourse and more popular ecological discourse. To whatever degree hostility between species (or competition) drives biological development notwithstanding, the development of species vis-à-vis other species and ecosystems is hardly unnatural within popular discourse. Indeed, there may be a debate about specific dynamics and nuanced relationships, but it's hardly unnatural. Rather, according to popular ecological discourse, this is simply the way things are. Indeed, popular discourse agrees with orthodox theology in the sense that humanity has exhibited a particular propensity to muck it all up, but to say

---

12. The Hebrew reads *mōra ʾăkem weḥitte̊kem*, which is a nominal hendiadys. This grammatical construction presents a singular thought through the conjoining of two or more words. It's often used for emphasis. Arnold and Choi, *Guide to Biblical Hebrew Syntax*, 158–59.

13. For a sustained treatment of this, see Richter, *Epic of Eden*.

that creation is so fundamentally dysfunctional that it can only be rectified by supernatural action at some point in an undetermined future is very different. Make no mistake about it, orthodox Christian theology argues that the created order will not be brought back to its intended state, its natural state, short of the culmination of a divinely ordained plan. So, again, I'm back to the question that's driving this project: to what degree are these conversations compatible?

6

A Sleeping Lion and a Changing World

MANY THOUSANDS OF YEARS ago, there was a volcanic event off the northwest coast of San Cristóbal Island. When that hot spot erupted, the magma mixed with the saltwater and set off an instantaneous chain reaction that resulted in a bomb-like explosion that catapulted ash and rock high into the air only to fall back down and settle in the shape of a cone. But after thousands of years of wind and rain erosion, that cone has assumed the very crude shape of a sleeping lion, or as they call it, Leon Dormido. It's also known as Kicker Rock.

Kicker Rock.

Kicker Rock has become one of the most popular snorkeling destinations in the archipelago. It really doesn't matter which island you are on. If you are walking by one of the copious excursion brokers, they undoubtedly will have a picture of Kicker Rock trying to sell you an excursion. It's popular for a number of reasons. It's a bastion of hammerhead sharks when the water is warm. Sea turtles—big sea turtles, for that matter—are always present. And then there are many species of tropical fish that hover around the base of the rock looking for food. But what is arguably the most interesting element of the rock is the large crevice that features toward one end of the rock formation. You can snorkel into the large gap in the rock and swim into the interior of the formation. It's a bit unsettling, particularly if you're claustrophobic. But it was in that gap that I saw my first whitetip shark swimming in the opposite direction about ten feet below me.

On both trips to the Galápagos Islands, Ginny and I went snorkeling there. Yet, while both trips couldn't have been more different, both trips were some of the most surreal experiences of my life. During our first trip, we were part of a medium-sized excursion group populated by snorkelers and scuba divers. Truth be told, it was a very eclectic group. There were young couples from Latin America, a young couple from England who had been scuba diving all over the world, and even unfit Americans with the propensity to get seasick. Yet, despite the group's diversity, when the boat stopped, we lined up and uniformly jumped into the ocean. As soon as I hit the water, gathered my wits, and looked down, I saw five massive Eastern Pacific green sea turtles swimming at various depths below me. The diameters of the shells varied as well, but some of them were almost four feet in diameter.

A Pacific Green Sea Turtle.

Frigatebirds, Sea Lions, and Darwin

Boy, were they graceful swimmers, effortlessly paddling and gliding through the abnormally warm water. And there were also countless tropical fish, big and small, swimming in large schools and smaller groups. Oh yeah, there was also the sea lion bobbing in the water feasting on the carcass of some dead animal.

We also were fortunate enough to see hammerhead sharks, which were more difficult to see. Yet, between the snorkeling guides diving below the surface only to come up pounding the sides of their heads yelling, "Hammerhead," and the discernible T-shaped head on a large fish-like creature, I can confidently say that I "saw" a fully grown hammerhead shark in the wild. Besides, the scuba divers that were on our charter claimed that a large group of hammerheads got within arm's length when they were doing whatever scuba divers do at the base of the rock.

On the 2023 trip, we snorkeled for about ninety minutes, and it seemed like time flew by. However, in 2024, we snorkeled for about the same time, but the time drug on. Truth be told, the 2024 trip was not nearly as exciting. Sure, there were the tropical fish and the Eastern Pacific sea turtles—and it's always invigorating to be swimming in the open ocean. But there were no shark encounters, nor was the water as clear or visible. It was a bit disappointing, if I am completely honest. However, the more I reflected upon the very different 2024 trip, I have come to temper my disappointment. The conditions were completely different.

Most fundamentally, the water was colder on the 2024 trip. I mean, *significantly* colder. In fact, it was a shock to our system when we jumped it, taking our breath away for a moment. While we eventually warmed up, it was still unwise to stay still for very long. In addition, there was a swell in the ocean current that swirled around various kinds of sea sediment and therefore dramatically decreased visibility. Yet, despite these differing variables, we were able to spend several hours during both trips at a pristine and isolated beach adjacent to Kicker Rock: Cerro Brujo. I mentioned this site earlier as the place where our snorkeling guide appeared annoyed with my fascination with the frigatebird. However, my interaction there with our tour guide in 2023 went beyond a discussion of the frigatebird. We also spoke about one of the most iconic animals in the archipelago—the marine iguana. Specifically, we discussed the relationship between the iguana and El Niño.

A Marine Iguana on Cerro Brujo.

When we were in Ecuador in 2023 at the end of May and the beginning of June, what appeared to be El Niño was unexpectedly affecting the region. Because the waters were significantly warmer than expected, many people were suggesting that these currents were the product of an unpredicted El Niño event. Now when I hear the term "El Niño," I very quickly think of a young Chris Farley waiving his arms wildly while wearing a flamboyant sequined outfit and proclaiming, "I'm El Niño! It's Spanish for [long pause] 'The Niño!'" However, as silly as that *Saturday Night Live* skit was, El Niño is a real, regularly recurring climatological phenomenon that has wide-ranging implications. Specific to the Galápagos Islands, El Niño prevents cold water currents from circulating nutrients from deeper ocean levels, which happens to be critical for the satiation of marine life. And specific to the marine iguanas, El

Niño has a particularly devastating effect. Estimates suggest that 60 to 70 percent of the population could die in a particularly hard El Niño summer. Some estimates even project a higher mortality. Why such a high rate of death? The warm water currents ruin the algae crop that is critical to the iguana population. And without the necessary nutrients in the algae, the iguanas essentially starve. If they do survive, they survive with a dramatically reduced weight and body composition.

By June 2023, several weeks after our visit, world meteorological associations verified that El Niño had unexpectedly gripped the region.[1] Thus, the 2023 summer became a summer when the highly vulnerable marine iguana was forced to adopt certain austerity measures to facilitate survival. And when we returned in 2024, my impression was that the marine iguanas were not as ubiquitous. They were not lying in piles, sunning themselves on the beaches of La Loberias on San Cristóbal or on Avenue Charles Darwin in Puerto Ayora on Santa Cruz. And the ones that we did see were significantly smaller.

El Niño functions with La Niña as a type of hot water/cold water partnership. They don't appear together, but they tend to oscillate in predictable cycles, bringing hot- and cold-water currents into the archipelago. Again, this was the issue of debate in 2023. There was the anticipation of La Niña only to get a visit from El Niño. And so, island natives, tourists, and researchers all noticed certain symptoms, such as the abnormally warmer currents and the slower transition of seasons, and were trying to put their collective fingers on the reason. I distinctly remember in 2023 asking our guide on Cerro Brujo about the possibility of an El Niño summer only to be rebuffed by the statement that the national park services were not ready to label what they were seeing as an El Niño summer. But even more telling, in that conversation, a phrase was thrown about that has often been understood as profanity among many conservative Christians: climate change.

---

1. For a very telling visualization and discussion of this transition, see Becker, "August 2023 El Niño Update." For the visual in isolation, see https://www.climate.gov/media/15516.

"Climate change" is a term that produces strong opinions on all sides of the ideological debate. Speaking in generalities, you've either drunk the Kool-Aid of liberal, quasi-communist propaganda or you're an uncouth Neanderthal that denies science. Moreover, traditionally, there has been a sharp dichotomy between camps. Even in the modern American church, I struggle to see any irenic debate. Indeed, the landscape is changing, but the traditional black-and-white dichotomy is still very much alive. Yet, basic observations between the summers of 2023 and 2024 tell me that the population and size of the marine iguanas were noticeably different. In 2024, it was as if the biggest iguanas had decided to swim to another archipelago. And when I consider the most obvious difference, the remarkably colder water temperatures, our experiences tell me that climate change is a real thing and that it deeply affects ecosystems.

In 2024, our family added the island of Isabela to our itinerary. Instead of hopping between Santa Cruz and San Cristóbal, we boarded a water ferry on Santa Cruz and headed farther west to the largest island in the archipelago: Isabela. At over 1700 square miles, it's been made from the fusion of six shield volcanos, arguably the most famous of which is Sierra Negra. Negra is a popular tourist site, but it does involve a fair amount of hiking to get up the rim of the caldera. The main city on the island is Puerto Villamil and is the home to virtually all the island's population. While the number of hotels and restaurants continues to increase yearly, Villamil and Isabela have a distinctly different feel than the other islands and cities, respectively. Many of the roads are dirt or sand, and the "hustle" of Puerto Ayaro is replaced by bikes, walkers, and the constant crashing of the waves on the beach.

Undoubtedly, Isabela is most famous for its active volcanoes, the presence of Galápagos tortoises wandering unencumbered in the wild, and the very unique Galápagos penguin (*Spheniscus mendiculus*). In fact, as you approach the main bay of Isabela, you will likely get a close-up view of one of the most peculiar species in the animal kingdom. Penguins at the equator are still something that is hard to comprehend.

These penguins populate the port of Villamil, swimming at rapid speeds through the calm, clear water. They also hang out on the rocks that line the port alongside pelicans and blue-footed boobies. Their calm and cool demeanor is interrupted occasionally by the urge to cool off and/or fish. In fact, Ginny and I were fortunate enough to observe this on a kayak tour throughout the harbor. We saw them standing there, slowly moving their heads from side to side as they scanned the water, only to unpredictably fall into the water and dart through it at almost lightning speeds. These cute (but very fast) birds are beyond a doubt a marvel of the island chain. However, the species is dying at an alarming rate.

A Sleeping Lion and a Changing World

Blue-Footed Boobies, Galápagos Penguins, Galápagos Sea Lions in the Bay of Villamil.

The Galápagos penguins only lay one egg at a time, and when that egg is laid, both parents must take turns guarding the egg, often by standing over top of the egg. Yet this is the equator. It's always hot. So, eventually, the adult guarding the egg will have to get into the water to cool off. When this happens, the egg becomes extremely vulnerable to predators, not to mention the heat. Thus, in many instances, the egg is either eaten or cooked. Truth be told, it's a highly inefficient reproductive system. Moreover, the mortality rate of the Galápagos penguin is outpacing the species' ability to reproduce. To put it crudely, *Spheniscus mendiculus* exhibits a negative growth trend, and perhaps more than any other creature endemic to the Galápagos, the Galápagos penguin symbolizes the ongoing changes to the animal kingdom.

Geologically, the archipelago is also changing. When we visited in 2024, the very active La Cumbre shield volcano was erupting on Fernandina, a smaller, virtually undeveloped island. Through the Internet, the Ecuadorian government offered real-time footage of the volcanic process that formed the islands of the Galápagos millions of years ago. One could see the lava erupting, moving, and settling to eventually harden as the molten rock reached the sea. All of this ultimately increases the terrestrial footprint of Fernandina, which will also spur on further ecological possibilities.

If I can be completely transparent, the talking points surrounding climate change in the circles in which I grew up blow my mind. I don't understand them. You just have to spend enough time in various natural environments in various parts of the world to realize that ecological landscapes are not only changing but also losing some of their iconic elements. I am thinking about the Old Man of the Mountain (a.k.a. the Great Stone Face or the Profile) that collapsed in 2003, depriving New Hampshire of one of its most iconic terrestrial features. There's also the well-known glacial retreat in Kenai Fjords National Park. Even more intricately, the United States National Park Service maintains that the three-degree increase in temperature over the past century has resulted in shorter winters and longer summers, which in turn produces the melting of snowcaps two to three weeks earlier.[2] This accelerated melting alters the blooming of spring flowers and ensures that pine beetles will have more time to alter the terrain by destroying pine forests.

Have you ever seen a mountainside painted brownish-grey by dead pine trees?

Similarly, the warming temperatures in the Greater Yellowstone Ecosystem reduce the snowpack and the volume of the spring melt. This is critical as this runoff feeds into the Yellowstone, Snake, and Green Rivers, all of which have their genesis in the Greater Yellowstone Ecosystem and function as structures for drinking water, agriculture, and recreation. Warming temperatures in the Greater Yellowstone Ecosystem also contribute to wildfires

---

2. National Park Service, "Climate Change, Rocky Mountain National Park." For a catalog of publications that inform the NPS's position and response to climate change, see National Park Service, "Park-Specific Climate Change."

and insect infestations.[3] Elsewhere, the reduction in snowpacks negatively impacts tundra environments that function as critical habitats for impressive mammals, like the arctic fox and polar bear. I could go on and on, but hopefully you get the point.

While such scenarios appear pretty straightforward, debate is intense on the role of human agency and the government for facilitating change. Only a belligerent ideologue would argue that humanity is not a culpable agent with their burning of fossil fuels, the reduction of pristine habitats, or other destructive habits. But the degree at which the government steps in to force climate-friendly initiatives is a legitimate conversation. On the one hand, the impression that Bill Nye gives in both *Undeniable* and *Unstoppable* is a bit over the top. But to pretend that the government should not have a role to play in shaping policy is similarly naive. Left to our own devices, humanity struggles to change. We tend to need some type of stimulus. Yet to become passive and allow an outside agent to dictate invites a whole new set of questions. A balance needs to be struck. Unfortunately, as I write this, such a balance appears to be a pipe dream. The American political system is so fractured that the United States Congress struggles to pass basic bills. Recently reelected President Trump is once again threatening to pull out of global climate agreements, and Congress is poised for gridlock as the president-elect advocates for economic stability under the mantra, "Drill baby, drill!"

---

3. National Park Service, "Climate Change, Yellowstone."

Frigatebirds, Sea Lions, and Darwin

I remember reading Sandra Richter's *Epic of Eden* and coming to a realization that a healthy view of the Bible's message of salvation requires an awareness that the original intentions of God's creation were not abandoned on the heels of humanity's original missteps. Rather, as part of the entire salvation process, those creative intentions are to be redeemed, or brought back in line with divine intentions. As Richter is fond of saying, "What began in Eden, ends in Eden."[4] The implication of this simple statement eventually hit me like a 2x4 to the back of the head. I realized that Christians should not only be concerned with their ecological context, but they should advocate for policies and practices that curb the unnecessary degradation of their ecological contexts and unbridled consumerism. Now, I am not saying that you have to change your entire ideological foundation because of this realization, but this is very different than the stereotyped presentations I was fed growing up. They essentially went like this: "People who advocate for conservation are hippies, tree huggers . . . Democrats. And being a conservative Republican Christian, we don't support Democratic policies."

4. Richter has a habit of saying this phrase in her lectures, the essence of which is articulated in Richter, *Epic of Eden*, 119–36.

Consequently, you can see the problem. Where I grew up, climate change and ecology were political footballs. Some groups would take those footballs and run with them, making them a foundational staple to their political positions. Other groups would mock Greta Thunberg as a naive child detached from the real world, only to eventually punt the football. They were not interested in issues that detracted from certain moral responsibilities and economic realities. And if you dared to deviate, then you would be chastised. Indeed, what I experienced in those moments when I was reading Richter's *Epic of Eden* is hardly unique. In fact, you may have had a similar experience. But there's something about spending over a week in an iconic, pristine environment, watching animals you otherwise only see on the National Geographic channel, that stimulates this realization and encourages you to take issues of climate change more seriously. Perhaps they may convince you to embrace any evolving convictions that you may sense developing.

7

Water Ferries, Economics, and the Problem with Tourists

ONE OF THE LOGISTICAL hurdles that you have to navigate when you are traveling through the archipelago is how to get to the different islands. Essentially, you have two options. Option one is to fly. Option two is to take what's called a water ferry. If you're richer than Croesus, then flying is a viable option. Tickets for each passenger are well over one hundred dollars, and there are also tight regulations for baggage. Alternatively, the more economical method of transportation between islands—by a long shot—is to get a chartered boat for about thirty-five dollars a head with about thirty other people, cram yourselves into the interior of the boat, and enjoy a relatively bumpy ride across the Pacific Ocean for about two hours.

Now... this is an experience! I will never forget my first water ferry ride between San Cristóbal and Santa Cruz. We had taken the afternoon ferry for reasons I no longer remember, so it was hot. I mean really hot. Of course, this general discomfort was exacerbated by having to stand on the dock, in the sun, with minimal hydration. Now you may ask, "Why not drink all the water you need?" Well, it's because of what's called the "ship's head." This refers to a solitary toilet, located in a very small cabin at the front of the boat, often closed off by a door that either doesn't shut well or will easily fly open if the boat hits a big enough wave. It's supposed to be reserved for emergencies, which was reinforced by my brother-in-law as we prepared for that first ride. In fact, Ben was extremely adamant that if there was an emergency bathroom situation, we should just go to the bathroom in our pants instead of using the ship's head. When he breached this subject with my daughters, the conversation went something like this:

"OK, girls. We need to talk about something really serious."

"What's that, Uncle Ben? We have all the things packed. We haven't really eaten in a while. And we've taken our Dramamine."

"It's about the potty . . . on the boat."

"Is there a potty on the boat?"

"Yes, but you can't use it."

"What do you mean we can't use it? What if we have to go to the bathroom?"

"If you have to go to the bathroom, you need to hold it. You can't use the bathroom."

"Is it broken? Why can't we use the bathroom if we need to go?"

"It would be better to cast yourself into the sea than have to use the ship's head."

Ben went on to describe to the kids that if you had to use that potty, you would bounce everywhere while sitting on the potty. And as you bounced around, you would finish your business in a less-than-controlled manner. In Ben's mind, this was the most disgusting scenario that he could like of. Envisioning one of his nieces trying to go to the bathroom as they bounced around the cabin was too much to bear, particularly for his strict sensibilities regarding hygiene.

Truth be told, I watched this scenario unfold during our commute from Santa Cruz to Isabela during our 2024 trip. There was a man who made three different trips to the ship's head as we traversed the Pacific Ocean. Not one . . . or two. Three! And with each trip, his pants grew increasingly wetter. I knew this because he walked right past me on his walk of shame. I looked on in utter amazement as this guy, seemingly unashamed, continued to visit this toilet in full view of all the passengers, as if to say, "Yep! I can't hold it!" His urges even forced the boat to stop in the middle of the Pacific. We just sat there, bobbing like a cork, as this guy used the restroom.

In spite of this, these water ferry trips can be remarkably tranquil. The loud hum of the outboard motors can serenade you to sleep if the ocean is smooth enough. And you can even get a good view of dolphins swimming and playing in the wake of the boats as they speed by. And the experience of traveling over open ocean, where you will eventually lose sight of all land, leaves an indelible mark. You come to appreciate anew the beauty of the maritime world as the sun reflects brightly off the glassy sea and you catch a glimpse of a dolphin's arched back as it glides through the water.

But make no mistake, there's an entire industry that has developed around these ferry rides. You have vendors who hock their tickets and boats as you walk along the main drags of the port cities. And you've got to be careful, because over-booking and illegitimate tickets are always a possibility. But when you show up on the dock, your luggage will be checked by local authorities manning an airport-like X-ray machine right before you have to pay a dock fee. It's not much, but it's about one dollar per person. Once you're on the dock, you wait until your boat is called by the supervisor and the Ecuadorian navy. When it's called, you leave your luggage and get into what's called a water taxi, which is a small boat with a relatively small outboard motor that takes you from the dock to your chartered boat somewhere in the harbor. Oh yes, you have to pay for the water taxi as well. It's only a dollar, but after a while, you do get the feeling that everyone is nickeling-and-diming you to death.

Water Ferries, Economics, and the Problem with Tourists

As for the water-taxi rides to the ferry, they are always peaceful. In fact, this is a short period of time where you can see a lot of neat wildlife up close. Sea lions lie on the dock, blocking your way to ramps and boats. These things are so massive that you can't just scurry them away. *You* have to walk around *them*. But you will also see them from the boat, swimming right by the taxi. You will also see pelicans fly just outside your arm's reach as sea turtles break the water's surface to get a breath of air. If you're really lucky, you can see something even more exotic. I remember in 2023, while we were standing on the dock in Puerto Ayora waiting for our water ferry to go back to San Cristóbal, I saw a huge spotted eagle ray swimming through the harbor about one foot below the surface. The wingspan on this ray had to be at least six feet, and it effortlessly cut through the water. But by the time I got Ginny's attention to show her, it was essentially gone. She only got a quick glimpse of it.

Tourism in the Galápagos Islands is built on the back of these types of industries. The reality is that if these networks of ferries neither existed nor had the support from the local dock workers, boat people, and government, transport between islands would be essentially impossible. And if transportation between islands were restricted, then the general appeal of the archipelago would evaporate. Sure, cruise ships would still sail through the archipelago, making stops at various islands, but these trips are largely cost prohibitive for most families. Consequently, for all their logistical difficulties, the water ferries between San Cristóbal, Santa Cruz, and Isabela allow families to experience the islands. And truth be told, the issue of tourism has created something of a conundrum for the Galápagos Islands.

In August 2024, *The Guardian* shed light on the delicate balance between tourism and conservation. One particular article opened with a story of Carolina Proaña.[1] Reportedly, she had been trying to do her part to save the endangered Galápagos petrel (*Pterodroma phaeopygia*), a sea bird famous for ground nesting and returning to the same location year after year to lay their eggs. Her family owns land on Santa Cruz, and one portion of that land has become a recognized nesting ground for the Galápagos petrel. On one occasion, however, Proaña found two dead petrels immediately outside their nesting area. Initially dumbfounded by what she saw, she mined her motion camera setup to watch the birds and eventually determined that the culprits were two stray dogs. And while surveying these images of the resting site, she also saw a cat lurking around the area.

For the Galápagos, the issue of freely wandering cats and dogs has become a serious issue. I have spoken about this in a previous chapter, but it's worth repeating that these are introduced species linked to the increased settlement and tourism numbers. In short, as people are moving on to the island, they are bringing with them many domesticated species that ultimately pose a threat to the endemic species of the islands. Whether because of pathogens or through the introduction of new predators into the food chain, species like the petrel, marine iguana, and the blue-footed booby are facing new threats to their existence. And sadly, in many instances, the endemic species are losing. Even bugs and

1. Brown, "Problem with People."

other insects imported onto the island via shipping containers and other imports are having an adverse effect on many animal populations. For example, it's well known that the vampire fly (*Philornis downsi*) has eviscerated certain avian populations.[2]

Apparently, the rise in tourism and settlement numbers also has an adverse effect on water management. In 2023, there were approximately 330,000 visitors to the Galápagos Islands. As a point of reference, such a figure would put the Galápagos Island National Park between 49 and 50 on the list of most-visited national parks in the United States, falling between Pinnacles National Park and the Channel Islands National Park.[3] This doesn't seem like a very high figure, but compared to the 30,000 people that live on the islands, it's clear that tourism overwhelms the island chain. Consequently, as one would expect, sewage and runoff systems can't keep up. Thus, it's normal that contaminated water often makes its way into the harbors and oceans. In Puerto Ayora, one is reminded of this with every rainstorm. In no time at all, rainwater mixes with oil from cars and buses, discarded banana peels, and even small amounts of animal excrement only to flow intensely down the main street toward the harbor. In many places, water pools by the curbs and crosswalks, constructing a nice bath for your feet if you're not paying attention. Even landfills are overrun with garbage, eventually creating garbage mountains that accentuate the naturally occurring highlands in the interior of the islands.

---

2. Galápagos Conservancy, "Protecting Landbirds"; Galápagos Conservation Trust, "Avian Vampire Fly."

3. National Park Service, "Annual Park Ranking for Recreational Visits 2023."

Frigatebirds, Sea Lions, and Darwin

A Marine Iguana Lying on Lava Rocks with Some Sally Lightfoot Crabs.

If you are reading this, and you are starting to imagine a city like seventeenth-century Paris or the slums of Mumbai, please don't. I am exaggerating a bit here. However, it hopefully illustrates the point that I am trying to make. While tourism is the economic lifeblood of these islands, the sheer popularity of this place is pushing the limits of the archipelago's infrastructure. Overwhelmingly, the inhabitants, particularly those that live in the cities, in one way or another service the tourism industry. Whether it's functioning as a guide, running a local eatery or trinket shop, or brokering tours, the people of Santa Cruz, San Cristóbal, and other islands have come to rely on these transient populations. But every person and every shipment onto the island brings with it the possibility of one more invasive species that could fundamentally alter the Galápagos ecosystem.

So, at the expense of sounding glib, it's useful to invoke the *Guardian* article referenced above to summarize the delicate situation that defines daily life on the islands.

The Galápagos Islands National Park controls 97 percent of land in the archipelago, meaning that 30,000 inhabitants live on only 3 percent of the land. And because virtually all these people serve the tourism industry, the inhabitants of the Galápagos *need* outsiders. They need people to come to their towns, rent boats, go on snorkeling tours, take ferries to other islands, buy trinkets, and eat at their restaurants. However, with each outsider comes the possibility of invasive species being introduced into the ecosystem.[4] Indeed, there's a logistically awkward bio-screening process to which all tourists must subject themselves, but that process can't catch all potential insurgents. What's more, anyone who relies on tourism knows that money is incredibly fickle. In fact, the *Guardian* article notes the dramatic downturn in tourism dollars between 2023 and 2024,[5] which means that those valuable tourism dollars must be allocated by the government in extremely effective ways to not only increase the quality of life but also reinforce important ecological programs. In other words, life in the Galápagos is a bit ironic. The thing upon which the Galápagos Islands relies is one of the things that threatens its famously pristine ecosystem.

Nicolette Reale has described this as an "economic and ecological paradox,"[6] and Elizabeth Hennessy has summed this up while talking about the iconic Galápagos tortoises:

> Tourism to this bucket-list destination generates much of the funding for conservation. [The iconic Galápagos tortoise Lonesome] George and other animals are valuable commodities for an industry that sells visitors the opportunity to get close to wildlife known for being unfazed by the presence of humans.... The local economy is booming—from the late 1990s to the 2000s, the islands' annual economic growth rate was an astounding 78 percent, making them one of the fastest growing economies in the world and a significant source of revenue for the

---

4. There are well-documented cases of rats, goats, boars, and other species being introduced into the islands that led to virtual eradication of the Galápagos tortoises. Only through a systematic and aggressive campaign against such species have the Galápagos tortoises been able to rebound and thrive. Hennessy, *On the Backs of Tortoises*, 7.

5. Brown, "Problem with People."

6. Reale, "Galápagos Islands."

Frigatebirds, Sea Lions, and Darwin

Ecuadorian state. But this alliance between tourism and conservation is uneasy. There are downsides to iconic charisma: the booming industry also brings with it a host of issues that threaten conservation, including a rapidly growing human population that has increased from about two thousand in 1960 to more than thirty thousand today. These island residents live in the 3 percent of the islands not included in the national park. Supporting them—and tourists—means importing from the continent everything from food to air conditioners to fuel. With the increased transportation that brings people and goods to the archipelago also come foreign species and diseases. Conservationists and journalists alike fret about whether the Galápagos archipelago has become too successful for its own good, creating a crisis of overdevelopment in a place best known as an isolated sanctuary of nature.[7]

More broadly, there's an irony that surrounds ecological discourse. The discipline of science is best suited to inform the populace and shed light on various ecological issues that face humanity, whether in the short or long term. However, as noted by Brunner, Butler, and Swoboda, "For all the good that science has accomplished in our world, it has repeatedly failed to motivate the kind of expansive change needed to make a significant impact on the ecocrisis."[8] The obvious question is, why? Why can't science communicate and persuade effectively? They have Bill Nye, NPR, and Greta Thunberg. Is it politics? Yep. Is it general apathy, a willingness to kick the can down the road even more? Probably. Is it money, as changing so many things would be extremely expensive? For sure. And I would also say that it's also got to be linked to the problem of the ivory tower. Ecological research is extremely technical. You just have to listen to my brother-in-law for about two minutes to realize that the terms and processes that he infuses into his conversations require immense amounts of effort to comprehend. I often ask him to clarify and repeat himself

---

7. Hennessy, *On the Backs of Tortoises*, 12–13.
8. Brunner et al., *Introducing Evangelical Ecotheology*, 34.

during our discussions. And when you live in this highly technical and specialized world, making your living talking to people who similarly understand your specialized conversations, it's very difficult to switch that frame of reference to speak to the populace about the significance of your work.

In light of this, Brunner, Butler, and Swoboda have argued that Christianity is uniquely positioned to step into this vacuum to argue and persuade the populace about issues of conservation and ecology. In fact, this is the driving force behind their work *Introducing Evangelical Ecotheology*. They argue linguistically, conceptually, and based on God's character—all of which are argued to be scriptural—to create a theological and moral imperative. So, the divine mandate in Gen 2:15 for humanity to "keep" the garden of Eden establishes practical expectations.[9] And the primary theological framework for understanding Scripture—the covenant—assumes mutuality, exhorting humanity that it has skin in the game here. Quite simply, ecological commitments will benefit humanity as well.[10] Even the creativity of creation alongside the very character of the Creator elucidates foundational traits that should be in those who follow God Almighty.[11] Yet despite all of this, the unavoidable fact is that the church has displayed a complicated, perhaps ambiguous, relationship with ecological theory and discourse throughout its history.[12] In other words, there's another level to the irony of Christian ecological discourse when it comes to this issue: the ideology well-suited to carry the discarded mantle of science, to convince people of their moral prerogative for conservation and ecology, has proven to be inconsistent and lackadaisical.

Yet, I would like to believe that I am not naive, as if the ecological irony of the Galápagos Islands can be merely reduced to a lack of "illumination." To put it rather bluntly, the paradox is a

9. Brunner et al., *Introducing Evangelical Ecotheology*, 25–26.
10. Brunner et al., *Introducing Evangelical Ecotheology*, 26–27.
11. Brunner et al., *Introducing Evangelical Ecotheology*, 31–34.
12. For their survey, Brunner et al., *Introducing Evangelical Ecotheology*, 67–94.

present reality for the islands because of the economic potential. The *Guardian* article discussed throughout this chapter also interviewed Gunter Reck, a retired biology professor and co-director of the Institute of Applied Ecology at the Universidad of San Francisco de Quito, who argued that ecological considerations can't be the only thing driving the bus. He went on to explain that despite tourism's strain on the infrastructure, ecosystems have remained, and in some cases, they've been restored. The most famous example of this is the resurrection of the Galápagos tortoise populations on the archipelago.[13] More practically, there are countless stories of farmers, vendors, and restaurant owners taking massive economic hits due to drops in tourism revenue. So, in the end, it's a very complicated mess. There are lot of moving pieces and different considerations.

---

13. For more information, see Hennessy, *On the Backs of Tortoises*.

8

Wrapping Up These Musings

IN THE WAKE OF our trips to the islands, on several occasions I have reflected upon my shifting positions on issues of creation, ecology, and evolution. To put it simply, I'm currently at the point where I think my developments on these issues correspond to larger trends in my intellectual development. The reality is that when you grow up in northwest Ohio, where you can see corn and soybeans all the way to the horizon, life tends to be straightforward and simple. Yet, this kind of life is also insulated and predictable. However, my formal education took me away from that rural context and eventually sat me down in years of specialized study. This ultimately ended up with me obtaining a terminal research degree. You see, all this specialization exposed me to a more nuanced intellectual landscape versus the rather black-and-white landscape that I grew up in. Hermeneutically speaking, I'm more in tune with the semantic, cultural, and literary nuances of biblical interpretation than I was when I was eighteen years old, although I tend to think that despite this move toward a more nuanced position on things, I have kept a firm conviction that the Bible is God's word, clear in its plain sense, and strong in the assertions it makes.

Again, it's worth repeating: I'm proud of that simple, rural heritage. I don't believe it set me up to fail or that it constructed a façade where "deconstruction" was necessary for my spiritual or emotional health. Neither did it handicap me intellectually. The truth is that there is virtually nothing I would trade from those years. I actually think it gave me the foundation to obtain that terminal degree, not to mention the construction of a strong moral compass and a deep appreciation for Scripture. Yet, as I have also said in these musings, that heritage wasn't poised to push me beyond the simple to the sophisticated. And ultimately, I think that these realizations speak to one of the more lasting impressions that have come out of our trips to the Galápagos Islands.

There are so many moving parts and considerations that should ultimately affect one's positions on ecology, creation, and evolution. Consequently, positions built upon a mantra like "the Bible says it, and so I believe it" cannot possibly accommodate all the considerations one must entertain to form a competent position.

But if I can be more precise for a moment, there are two more specific convictions that I am compelled to emphasize as I wrap up these musings. First, experiencing the Galápagos Islands and other pristine environments makes all the difference in the world. Something intimate happens when humans spend time in environments that do not have the marks of humanity's expansion and development. And while this connection is admittedly hard to quantify, it very acutely produces an antidote to apathy and indifference. Memories are not only created through these experiences as cognitive bookmarks, but they are also forged with powerful emotions. Remembering how our middle daughter was nipped on the lower leg by a sea lion conjures up feelings of protection and responsibility. Remembering my family staring at and listening to the waves crash against the volcanic rock at La Lobería on San Cristóbal invokes a sense of awe for the sea's power and humanity's diminutive stature when confronted with such things. The implication is that when you encounter or observe an ecological conversation, whether it is the Galápagos Islands or any other pristine environment that you've visited, you realize that in a small way, you've got some skin in the game. You've got a vested interest in it. And when you visit these locations multiple times, reliving the memories of past visits while making new ones, all this is intensified.

Growing up in northwest Ohio, my family would make regular visits to national parks, as well as a few other similar types of environments. While our options were restricted for a number of reasons, we frequented the Great Smoky Mountains National Park, Mammoth Cave National Park, and any beaches that were within driving distance. Ginny and I have continued this trend, which also happened to be shared by her family (they are big fans of Shenandoah National Park), but we have made it a point to make the national parks a feature of our vacations. I remember one spring break driving out to New Mexico and back just to experience places like White Sands, Carlsbad Caverns, Guadalupe Mountains, and Hot Springs. And so, whether it's through a massive road trip or a flight out to Denver, Colorado, to drive to Rocky Mountain National Park or Yellowstone, we want our kids to experience the places that have been shielded from the intense and aggressive growth of humanity. What's more, we are convinced that these experiences will foster a deeper appreciation of the Creator way more than a weekend at Disney World would.

Of course, it goes without saying that taking the family to the Galápagos Islands accomplished this. However, the trips of 2023 and 2024 also added the variable of allowing them to experience a place where one of the greatest cognitive developments in human history took root. It was there where the seeds of modern biology and ecology were planted. It was there where one of humanity's most influential minds honed his intellectual frameworks that eventually allowed him to articulate anew one of the mysteries of the created order. In short, Charles Darwin's research on the Galápagos Islands constitutes one of humanity's watershed moments in the intellectual developments of homo sapiens.

I don't think that I'm alone in these sentiments. Toward the end of Ken Burns's *The National Parks: America's Best Idea*, Dayton Duncan reminisces about his childhood vacations to the national parks, specifically how they left an indelible mark upon his memory. But what is particularly impactful was the segment when he recounts the moments when his children experienced similar connections and realizations. It's here when apathy and indifference fail to ensnare the next generation. They begin to see themselves as part of something bigger than themselves. And it's when people care that hope thrives.

The second lasting impression that arises from this project is just how complicated all this really is. Conservation agendas are great, but they will eventually collide with the practical realities of life. On the Galápagos Islands, this truth of life is crystallized in a very tangible way. Conservation collides with tourism. As a previous chapter discussed, the archipelago *needs* tourism, and tourism thrives on development. Yet, tourism and development will inevitably change the environment. To put it simply, the islands' biggest desire is also their biggest threat. And if this dance wasn't delicate enough, the role of humanity in conservation adds another layer to the complexity, particularly for Christians.

As surveyed in the opening chapters, many Christians believe that humanity is to be a featured agent in the care of creation. Why? Because it's our moral responsibility as the bearers of the divine image. Indeed, this Christian conviction is fundamental as it enjoys its impetus in our authoritative texts. Moreover, it's hard to ignore the statements in Gen 1 and 2, which emphasize that humanity was intended to be in harmonious relationship with all aspects of the created order. Such a harmony was supposed to define our species. So, if we have become confessing members of the Christian faith, then we must come to embody all aspects of what it means to be agents of God's redemptive plan. In other words, if we are Christians, we are expected to live a life that participates in God's actions to restore creation.

Yet at this point, I am compelled to return to the conversation I recalled at the beginning of this project, which pivoted with Ben's question of whether Christian ecology is really compatible with popular ecological discussions. After all of my musings, the answer to his contemplation appears rather complicated, particularly since the conversation is exacerbated by ideological convictions that are not shared by all people involved in the conversation. I really don't want to give the impression that I'm being elusive. But I just don't think that there's an easy answer here.

**A Galápagos Tortoise Crossing the Road Outside
of El Chato Ranch on Santa Cruz.**

If our trips to the Galápagos Islands have done anything for me, they have clarified the paradox that faces any ecological program, particularly in the developing world. Conservation is great, and I think in a vacuum, everyone would be on board with saving natural resources, preserving pristine environments, reintroducing indigenous animal populations, restoring natural grasslands and forests, etc. Very few people, I think, would rather stare at a concrete jungle than take in natural landscapes. However, when efforts to preserve things encroach upon one's quality or ease of life, this is where the rubber meets the road. This is when conservation gets hard. For example, trash on the Galápagos Islands is a fairly complicated thing. It's not just a question of "what's trash and what's recyclable." You must decide whether it's trash, compost, or recyclable. Now, if you grew up on the islands, these decisions are likely ingrained into your thought process, and all of this is just second nature. However, as a visitor, you repeatedly go through a mental exercise as you stare at the three colored-coded trash cans juxtaposed to each other for at least thirty seconds as you try to figure out if your conclusion will align with the Ecuadorian government. But with all this said, economics is a massive source of friction for any conservation program. In a previous chapter, the issue of economic development for the betterment of daily life versus conservation programs has proven to be a central topic of conversation on the islands. Yet, this is not unique to the Galápagos Islands. For example, as I write these final musings at a coffee shop in Islamorada, Florida, a fight is brewing between the state government and the local municipalities over the issue of building permits. For decades, the Florida Keys has navigated a delicate dance over how many buildings can be constructed. Approval is subject to an equation that considers population increases, general economic need, ecological considerations, and an ability to completely evacuate the Keys within twenty-four hours in the event of a natural disaster. This week, *The Keys Weekly* continued its documentation of this long saga.[1] As it stands, local governments disapproved of the state's decision not to alter its official position on approving new building permits. Local governments essentially argued that current housing needs should compel the state to bring forward their normal yearly allocation months in advance. However, the state's response was to urge local municipalities to allocate their normal allotment before asking for more to be brought forward. You don't have to read too long in these articles to sense the strong opinions that dominate the conversation.

And speaking of strong opinions, they, along with the strong personalities that accompany them, tend to dominate the conversation, particularly in Christian circles. However, if I've learned anything, stubborn ideologues absolutely destroy any chance for irenic conversation. A great example of this phenomenon can be seen in the famous Ken Ham versus Bill Nye debate that was

---

1. Rickert, "What's the Magic Number?"; Rickert, "Marathon Council Set"; McCarthy, "Islamorada Council"; McCarthy, "'Oh Heck'"; Rickert, "Monroe County Commission."

originally broadcast on YouTube.[2] I have mentioned both people already, but it's worth repeating that both individuals have a palpable annoyance with people who do not fall into their ideological camp. Admittedly, Nye's annoyance seems to be more localized, focused on people like Ken Ham who are perceived to be intellectual Neanderthals because of their faith. But Ham's annoyance is more frustrating to me as a Christian. Ham focuses his criticisms on anyone who does not believe in what's called Young Earth creationism, regardless of your faith commitment (or lack thereof). Nevertheless, I digress.

When these two faced off in their much-anticipated debate, it landed with a ton of criticism.[3] Many questioned the usefulness of the debate, and there was a sense that they just talked past each other, emphasizing their own ideological convictions at the expense of any substantive debate.

Now this is not to suggest that I think Christians should take part in these ecological and scientific conversations with our biggest asset relegated to the sideline. I firmly believe our biggest asset in the conversation is our moral conviction that we should advocate for conservation and responsible engagement with the created order. Consequently, in this sense, I don't think that I can agree with my brother-in-law's latent frustration that became palpable as we talked at the Playa de la Estacion on Santa Cruz. I am not sure there's an inherent deficiency to Christians taking part in these conversations. In fact, I do think that our convictions can exhort and spur on conservation to a degree that science is incapable of achieving. Nevertheless, I do think that he was right to imply that playing the creation-care card as some type of trump card to ensure an audience and respect may be a bit foolish. The fact is that Christianity's conviction that humanity enjoys a privileged role in our care for creation is rooted in a set of texts that many scientists believe are mythical nonsense. Indeed, there are

2. Answers in Genesis, "Bill Nye Debates Ken Ham."
3. For a synopsis derived from real-time online interaction through a variety of social media platforms, as well as links to further opinions, see Chappell, "Who 'Won.'"

many well-respected scientists that are known to subscribe to the Christian faith, and many of these scientists have publicly written about their journey. Francis Collins is perhaps the most famous example.[4] But in every case, these scientists recognize that our authoritative texts must be understood in light of prescientific and culturally specific conceptual categories and literary conventions.

To put it another way, Christians need to understand the variables of what I call "convergence." We need to be more nuanced in understanding how our ecological conversations naturally converge—and diverge, for that matter—with modern scientific conservations so that we know when and how to persuade people to care. This is a drum that many biblical scholars have been pounding as of late. Whether it be in the form of a series produced by a single author that covers a variety of topics germane to these topics or in the form of an edited volume devoted to giving a platform for differing opinions (see opening chapters above), biblical scholarship appears to be reinvigorated around the notion that we need to understand what the Bible is actually saying and how that intersects with contemporary debates. And with all this said, I want to end with a few thoughts on how these convergences can inform the conversations. To accomplish this, I will rehash ideas and statements from chapter 4 above.

All discussion of creation, ecology, etc., are conditioned by an ancient Near Eastern worldview. The text employs well-known phrases and concepts that most modern minds would consider "mythical." Moreover, if you survey creation-speak across the ancient Near East, you will be hard-pressed to find anything truly unique or *sui generis*. Above all, when it comes to creation, it's discussed in terms of order, chaos, and function. That is, prior to creation, the world was in a disorderly or chaotic state, and it was out of this that creation established order and allocated functions to everything. Indeed, each culture in the ancient Near East had their own spin on the specifics, but this is the general dynamic driving all creation texts of ancient Israel's world. The implication is simple but very important: modern scientific, biological, and

---

4. Most famously, Collins, *Language of God*.

Wrapping Up These Musings

geological concepts go miles beyond the intended message of the text. Consequently, merging biblical statements about creation or the environment with modern ones, the latter of which are defined by incredibly technical jargon, can't be automatic or simplistic. You can't just take that ancient statement and "drop" it into modern conversations. Rather, there must be a process of evaluation whereby the reader of Scripture considers how these very different statements interact.

This process must begin with what the texts are trying to communicate. And if you recall from a previous chapter where I talk about the message of Gen 1–11, there are a number of linguistic, literary, and cultural elements to consider. But here it's worth repeating that the Bible's message of creation is equal parts polemical, simple, and imprecise. It's simple in the sense that the message of the creation texts clarifies that Yahweh is the divine Agent solely responsible for an orderly and functional creation. Humanity is the agent primarily responsible for messing up that "very good" feat. Yet, the Bible is relatively imprecise in the mechanisms of how this orderly and functional creation came to maturation. Now, one could indeed point to statements that God "said" things, that it transpired over a period of "days," and other things as evidence of the details. But you don't have to read too far into the research of these ancient Near Eastern cultures and their texts to see that each one of "details" is ironically imprecise and subject to pretty intimidating debate. Even the idea of God speaking things into existence has a parallel is the Memphite Theology of Egypt.[5] Consequently, at the end of the day, Christians need to admit that statements often marshalled as "details" are more astutely understood as evidence for the text's polemical nature. And this is really the driving force behind these texts more than telling us how the orderly and functional creation came to be. The Bible is concerned with debunking the popular notions of creation deeply rooted in the worldviews of the Iron Age and early Second Temple period. It is polemical, not scientific.

---

5. For this and other parallels throughout the opening chapters of Genesis, see Holland, "Enuma Elish," 19–40.

So, what do these realizations imply for the convergences between biblical discussions of creation and modern discussions that are defined by concepts incompatible with the thought-world of ancient Israel? Fundamentally, we have to accept that the Bible offers rather limited data points relevant to conversations about creation and evolution. For example, I mentioned the use of the causative verb stem in a previous chapter when talking about the creation texts of Gen 1. I suggested that this constituted textual license to at least entertain the place of evolution in one's paradigm of creation. Yet, any biblical instruction beyond this simple opportunity remains severely limited. Most fundamentally, the Bible is unashamedly clear that Yahweh *must be* the ultimate Agent behind any paradigm. He *must* be part of the equation... somehow... some way. This biblical mandate immediately handicaps any conversation mutually informed by the two camps. But even if the conversation can get past entertaining a variable that can't possibly be accommodated by one party, the Bible offers virtually nothing to the conversations about the biological relationships between species, how certain geographic features affect the adaptation of species, the age of the earth, or anything that dominates modern scientific research and discussion. Dare I say, to use the Bible in such scientific conversations asks it to bear a weight that it's not designed to bear.

The Bible's usefulness in ecological conversations, in my opinion, is more positive. Not from the standpoint of directly speaking to scientific facts that inform ecological debate, but rather, because it speaks to the ethical realities of conservation and ecological responsibility. In fact, it's worth rebeating a drum that I have beat at several points in this work. It is well positioned to argue for a responsible ethic because it anchors its advocacy in moral and theological convictions. Dare I say, the creation care advocated by the Bible is more than just a reasonably sound one. It strikes at the heart of who Christians claim to be. And to be completely transparent, I appreciate the work of biblical scholars like Sandra Richter who demonstrate through their interpretation of the biblical text, which is fundamentally informed by the cultural and historical contexts of the authors, that a concern for the environment is part and parcel with a commitment to following Jesus. Scholars like her have convinced me that these are things we can't fluff off.

Bibliography

Answers in Genesis. "Bill Nye Debates Ken Ham - HD (Official)." *YouTube*, February 4, 2014. https://www.youtube.com/watch?v=z6kgvhG3AkI.
Arnold, Bill T. *Encountering the Book of Genesis: A Study of Its Content and Issues*. Encountering Biblical Studies. Grand Rapids: Baker Academic, 1998.
———. "The Genesis Narratives." In *Ancient Israel's History: An Introduction to Issues and Sources*, edited by Bill T. Arnold and Richard S. Hess, 23–45. Grand Rapids: Baker Academic, 2014.
———. "Genesis 1 as Holiness Preamble." In *Let Us Go Up to Zion: Essays in Honour of H. G. M. Williamson on the Occasion of His Sixty-Fifth Birthday*, edited by Ian Provan and Mark J. Boda, 331–43. Leiden: Brill, 2012.
———. "Holiness Redaction of the Primeval History." *Zeitschrift für alttestamentliche Wissenschaft* 129.4 (2017) 483–500.
Arnold, Bill T., and Brian E. Beyer. *Encountering the Old Testament: A Christian Survey*. 4th Edition. Grand Rapids: Baker Academic, 2024.
Arnold, Bill T., and John H. Choi. *A Guide to Biblical Hebrew Syntax*. 2nd ed. Cambridge: Cambridge University Press, 2018.
Asbury Theological Seminary. "Our Statement of Faith." https://asburyseminary.edu/about/theological-orientation/statement-of-faith/.
Becker, Emily. "August 2023 El Niño Update: Back to School." *Climate.gov*, August 10, 2023. https://www.climate.gov/news-features/blogs/enso/august-2023-el-nino-update-back-school.
Botto-Mahan, Carezza, and Rodrigo Medel. "Was Chagas Disease Responsible for Darwin's Illness?: The Overlooked Eco-Epidemiological Context in Chile." *Revista Chilena de Historia Natural* 94.7 (2021) 1–7.
Brown, Kimberly. "The Problem with People: How More Tourists and a Growing Population are Taking Their Toll on the Galápagos Islands." *Guardian*, August 15, 2024. https://www.theguardian.com/global-development/

BIBLIOGRAPHY

article/2024/aug/15/dying-species-and-garbage-the-downsides-of-the-galapagos-tourism-dependency?CMP=share_btn_url.

Brunner, Daniel J., et al. *Introducing Evangelical Ecotheology: Foundations in Scripture, Theology, History, and Praxis*. Grand Rapids: Baker Academic, 2014.

Burch, William R., et al. *The Structure and Dynamics of Human Ecosystems: Toward a Model for Understanding and Action*. New Haven, CT: Yale University Press, 2017.

Burns, Ken, dir. *The National Parks: America's Best Idea*. Walpole, NH: Florentine Films, 2009.

Campbell, Anthony K., and Stephanie B. Matthews. "Darwin's Illness Revealed." *Postgraduate Medical Journal* 81 (2005) 248–51.

Chappell, Bill. "Who 'Won' the Creation vs. Evolution Debate?" *National Public Radio*, February 6, 2014. https://www.npr.org/sections/thetwo-way/2014/02/06/272535141/who-won-the-creation-vs-evolution-debate.

Collins, Francis S. *The Language of God: A Scientist Presents Evidence for Belief*. New York: Free, 2006.

Colp, Ralph, Jr. *Darwin's Illness*. Gainesville: University of Florida Press, 2008.

Darwin, Charles. "Letter No. 126." *Darwin Correspondence Project*. https://www.darwinproject.ac.uk/letter/?docId=letters/DCP-LETT-126.xml.

———. "Letter No. 144." *Darwin Correspondence Project*. https://www.darwinproject.ac.uk/letter/?docId=letters/DCP-LETT-144.xml.

———. "Letter No. 158." *Darwin Correspondence Project*. https://www.darwinproject.ac.uk/letter/?docId=letters/DCP-LETT-158.xml.

———. "Letter No. 159." *Darwin Correspondence Project*. https://www.darwinproject.ac.uk/letter/?docId=letters/DCP-LETT-159.xml.

———. "Letter No. 251." *Darwin Correspondence Project*. https://www.darwinproject.ac.uk/letter/?docId=letters/DCP-LETT-251.xml.

———. "Letter No. 259." *Darwin Correspondence Project*. https://www.darwinproject.ac.uk/letter/?docId=letters/DCP-LETT-259.xml.

———. *On the Origin of Species*. Oxford World Classics. Oxford: Oxford University Press, 2008.

———. *The Voyage of the Beagle*. The Harvard Classics. New York: P. F. Collier & Son, 1909.

Davidson, Gregg, and Kenneth J. Turner. *The Manifold Beauty of Genesis One: A Multi-Layered Approach*. Grand Rapids: Kregel Academic, 2021.

Denkinger, Judith, et al. "Urban Life of Galapagos Sea Lions (*Zalophus Wollebaeki*) on San Cristobol Island, Ecuador: Colony Trends and Threats." *Journal of Sea Research* 105 (2015) 10–14.

Elliott-Graves, Alkistis. "Ecology." *Stanford Encyclopedia of Philosophy*, February 21, 2024. Edited by Edward N. Zalta and Uri Nodelman. https://plato.stanford.edu/archives/spr2024/entries/ecology/.

Galápagos Conservancy. "Protecting Landbirds by Controlling the Avian Vampire Fly." www.galapagos.org/projects/rewilding-galapagos/biocontrol-of-the-avian-vampire-fly/.

BIBLIOGRAPHY

Galapagos Conservation Trust. "Avian Vampire Fly." https://galapagosconservation.org.uk/species/avian-vampire-fly/.

———. "Floreana." https://galapagosconservation.org.uk/about-galapagos/islands/floreana/.

———. "Global Relevance." https://galapagosconservation.org.uk/about-galapagos/global-relevance/.

Ham, Ken. "About." *Answers in Genesis*. https://answersingenesis.org/about/.

———. "History." *Answers in Genesis*. https://answersingenesis.org/about/history/.

Hamilton, Victor P. *The Book of Genesis, Chapters 1–17*. New International Commentary on the Old Testament. Grand Rapids: Eerdmans, 1990.

Hays, Christopher B. *Hidden Riches: A Sourcebook for the Comparative Study of the Hebrew Bible and Ancient Near East*. Louisville: Westminster John Knox, 2014.

Hennessy, Elizabeth. *On the Backs of Tortoises: Darwin, the Galapagos, and the Fate of Evolutionary Eden*. New Haven, CT: Yale University Press, 2019.

Hill, Carol, et al., eds. *The Grand Canyon: Monument to an Ancient Earth*. Grand Rapids: Kregel, 2016.

Holland, Drew S. "The Enuma Elish, the Memphite Theology, and Genesis 1: A Contextual Trialogue." In *Silhouettes of Scripture: Considering the Contextual Approach with Form Criticism*, 19–40. Lanham, MD: Lexington, 2023.

Houck, Oliver A. "Are Humans Part of Ecosystems?" *Environmental Law* 28.1 (1998) 3–4.

Indiana Wesleyan University. "University Profile." https://www.indwes.edu/about/profile/.

Jacobsen, Thorkild. *The Sumerian King List*. Chicago: University of Chicago Press, 1939.

Johnson, Drew. *What Hath Darwin to Do with Scripture?: Comparing the Conceptual World of the Bible and Evolution*. Downers Grove, IL: IVP Academic, 2023.

Johnson, Paul. *Darwin: Portrait of a Genius*. New York: Penguin, 2012.

Koehler, L., et al. *The Hebrew and Aramaic Lexicon of the Old Testament*. Translated by M. E. J. Richardson. 2 vols. Leiden: Brill, 2001.

Lamoureux, Denis O., et al. *Four Views on the Historical Adam*. Counterpoints. Grand Rapids: Zondervan Academic, 2013.

Leopold, Aldo. *A Sand County Almanac: And Sketches Here and There*. Oxford: Oxford University Press, 1949.

McCarthy, Jim. "Islamorada Council Could Repeal Previous Decision for More Building Requests." *Keys Weekly*, November 27, 2024. https://keysweekly.com/42/islamorada-council-could-repeal-previous-decision-for-more-building-permits/.

———. "Islamorada Council Majority Approves Ask for More Building Permits." *Keys Weekly*, December 12, 2024. https://keysweekly.com/42/islamorada-council-majority-approves-ask-for-more-building-permits/.

BIBLIOGRAPHY

———. "'Oh Heck': Tallahassee Isn't On Board with the County's Request for More Building Permits." *Keys Weekly*, December 12, 2024. https://keysweekly.com/42/oh-heck-tallahasee-isnt-on-board-with-countys-request-for-more-building-permits/.

McConnell, Robert L., and Daniel C. Abel. *Environmental Issues: An Introduction to Sustainability*. Upper Saddle River, NJ: Prentice Hall, 2008.

McDonnell, Mark J., and Steward T. A. Pickett, eds. *Humans as Components to Ecosystems: The Ecology of Subtle Human Effects and Populated Areas*. New York: Springer, 1993.

Miller, Joshua M., et al. "Genetic Pedigree Analysis of the Pilot Breeding Program for the Rediscovered Galapagos Giant Tortoise from Floreana Island." *Journal of Heredity* 109.6 (2018) 620–30.

Montagu, Joshua M. *Darwin: Competition and Cooperation*. New York: Henry Schuman, 1952.

Moo, Douglas, and Jonathan Moo. *Creation Care: A Biblical Theology of the Natural World*. Grand Rapids: Zondervan, 2018.

National Park Service. "Annual Park Ranking for Recreational Visits 2023." https://irma.nps.gov/Stats/SSRSReports/National%20Reports/Annual%20Park%20Ranking%20Report%20(1979%20-%20Last%20Calendar%20Year).

———. "Climate Change, Rocky Mountain National Park." https://www.nps.gov/romo/learn/nature/climatechange.htm.

———. "Climate Change, Yellowstone." https://www.nps.gov/yell/learn/nature/climatechange.htm.

———. "Park-Specific Climate Change." https://www.nps.gov/subjects/climatechange/parkclimatescience.htm.

Nelson, J. Bryan. *Pelicans, Cormorants, and Their Relatives: The Pelecaniformes*. Oxford: Oxford University Press, 2005.

Nelson, Paul, et al. *Three Views on Creation and Evolution*. Counterpoints. Grand Rapids: Zondervan, 1999.

Nowak, Martin A. "Five Rules for the Evolution of Cooperation." *Science* 314.5805 (2006) 1560–63.

Nye, Bill. *Undeniable: Evolution and the Science of Creation*. New York: St. Martin's, 2014.

———. *Unstoppable: Harnessing Science to Change the World*. New York: St. Martin's, 2015.

Orrego, Fernando, and Carlos Quintana. "Darwin's Illness: A Final Diagnosis." *Notes and Records of the Royal Society* 61.1 (2007) 23–29.

Oxford, Pete, and Graham Watkins. *Galapagos: Both Sides of the Coin*. Bournemouth: Imagine, 2009.

Reale, Nicolette. "The Galapagos Islands: Economy over Ecosystems." *Harvard International Review*, October 14, 2022. https://hir.harvard.edu/the-galapagos-islands-economy-over-ecosystems/.

Bibliography

Rickert, Alex. "Marathon Council Set to Decide Building Rights Request." *Keys Weekly*, November 7, 2024. https://keysweekly.com/42/marathon-council-set-to-decide-building-rights-request/.

———. "Marathon Workshop Packs the House as City Hones in on Building Rights Request." *Keys Weekly*, December 5, 2024. https://keysweekly.com/42/marathon-wokshop-packs-the-house-as-city-hones-in-on-building-rights-request/.

———. "Monroe County Commission Greenlights Building Right Request, Evacuation Time Change." *Keys Weekly*, December 20, 2024. https://keysweekly.com/42/monroe-county-commission-greenlights-building-right-request-evacuation-time-change/.

———. "What's the Magic Number?: County Leaders Begin Final Path to Building Rights Request." *Keys Weekly*, October 24, 2024. https://keysweekly.com/42/whats-the-magic-number-county-leaders-begin-final-path-to-building-rights-request/.

Richter, Sandra. *Epic of Eden: A Christian Entry into the Old Testament*. Downers Grove, IL: IVP Academic, 2008.

———. *Stewards of Eden: What Scripture Says about the Environment and Why It Matters*. Downers, Grove, IL: IVP Academic, 2020.

Ruiz-Saenz, Julian, et al. "Seroconversion in Galapagos Sea Lions (*Zalophus Wollebaeki*) Confirms the Presence of Canin Distemper Virus in Rookeries of San Cristobol Island." *Animals* 13.3657 (2023) 1–9.

Sarna, Nahum M. *Genesis*. JPS Torah Commentary. Philadelphia: Jewish Publication Society, 1989.

Schreiner, David B. *Pondering the Spade: Discussing Important Convergences between Archaeology and Old Testament Studies*. Eugene, OR: Wipf & Stock, 2019.

Sheehan, William, et al. "More on Darwin's Illness: Comment on the Final Diagnosis of Charles Darwin." *Notes and Records of the Royal Society* 62.2 (2008) 205–9.

Smith, Leo. *Ecology and Field Biology*. 5th ed. New York: HarperCollins, 1996.

"The Sumerian King List." *Livius.org*. https://www.livius.org/sources/content/anet/266-the-sumerian-king-list/.

Tigay, Jeffrey H. *The Evolution of the Gilgamesh Epic*. Wauconda, IL: Bolchazy-Carducci, 2002.

Vangemeren, W. A., ed. *New International Dictionary of Old Testament Theology and Exegesis*. 5 vols. Grand Rapids: Zondervan, 1997.

Walton, John H. *Ancient Near Eastern Thought and the Old Testament: Introducing the Conceptual World of the Hebrew Bible*. 2nd ed. Grand Rapids: Baker Academic, 2018.

———. *Genesis 1 as Ancient Cosmology*. Winona Lake, IN: Eisenbrauns, 2011.

———. "Interactions in the Ancient Cognitive Environment." In *Behind the Scenes of the Old Testament: Cultural, Social, and Historical Contexts*, edited by John S. Greer et al., 333–39. Grand Rapids: Baker Academic, 2018.

BIBLIOGRAPHY

———. *The Lost World of Genesis 1: Ancient Cosmology and the Origins Debate.* Downers Grove, IL: IVP Academic, 2009.

Young, D. A. B. "Darwin's Illness and Systematic Lupus Erythematosus." *Notes and Records of the Royal Society* 51.1 (1997) 77–86.

www.ingramcontent.com/pod-product-compliance
Lightning Source LLC
Chambersburg PA
CBHW071511150426
43191CB00009B/1486